THE LIVING WORD COMMENTARY

Editor
Everett Ferguson

Associate Editors
Abraham J. Malherbe · John David Stewart

The Second Letter
of Paul to
The Corinthians

The Second Letter of Paul to The Corinthians

James Thompson

πᾶσα γραφὴ
θεόπνευστος

R. B. SWEET CO., INC.

Austin, Texas

LIBRARY OF CONGRESS CATALOG CARD NUMBER: 75–113159

STANDARD BOOK NUMBER: 8344-0054-5

PRINTED IN U.S.A.

Acknowledgment

This commentary is based on the text of the Revised
Standard Version of the Bible, copyrighted 1946 and
1952 by the Division of Christian Education, National
Council of Churches, and used by permission.

Writers in *The Living Word Commentary* series have
been given freedom to develop their own understanding
of the biblical text. As long as a fair statement is given to
alternative interpretations, each writer has been per-
mitted to state his own conclusions. Beyond the general
editorial policies, the editors have sought no artificial
uniformity, and differences are allowed free expression.
A writer is responsible for his contribution alone, and
the views expressed are not necessarily the views of the
editors or publisher.

Contents

I

Introduction to Second Corinthians

PAUL'S RELATIONSHIP to the church at Corinth is more fully known than is his work with any other church that he founded. Luke records in Acts 18 the account of the founding of the Corinthian church. He states that Paul worked with the Corinthian church one year and six months (Acts 18:11). In addition, he reports that the response to the Christian message at Corinth was significant, as many Corinthians "hearing Paul believed and were baptized" (Acts 18:8).

The book of Acts leaves no more information about the condition of the Corinthian church subsequent to the account in Acts 18. It is from Paul's two letters to the Corinthians that one learns in most detail about the situation in the Corinthian church. Neither letter is a highly developed doctrinal discussion; instead, both are written to correct difficult situations within the Corinthian congregation. Thus the importance of these letters is in the portrait they give of an early Christian congregation. In these letters we get a glimpse of its worship, its doctrinal questions, and its points of controversy.

INTRODUCTION

Circumstances

Since Acts leaves no information about Paul's relationship to the Corinthians after the second missionary journey, one must infer from scattered remarks in the epistles themselves what situation lies behind the Corinthian epistles. From 1 Corinthians we learn of a previous letter Paul had sent to the Corinthians reprimanding the church for condoning immorality (1 Cor. 5:9). Paul wrote 1 Corinthians in response to a letter from the Corinthians in which he was asked to answer their questions (1 Cor. 7:1) with regard to marital questions (1 Cor. 7:1ff.), meats offered to idols (1 Cor. 8; 10), public worship (1 Cor. 14) and the resurrection (1 Cor. 15). In addition, he had received information from the household of Chloe that there were divisions in the Corinthian church (1:11).

Paul's second letter to the Corinthians is no mere continuation of the discussions of 1 Corinthians. In 2 Corinthians it is apparent that a whole new set of issues has been troubling the church there. It is equally obvious that between the writing of the two epistles the situation has changed remarkably. Paul indicates in 2 Corinthians 3:1 that visiting teachers, Jewish Christians who called themselves apostles and brought with themselves letters of recommendation, had worked to undermine the influence of Paul (see 11:4-6). Timothy had visited the Corinthians, evidently carrying with him 1 Corinthians (see 1 Cor. 16:10, 11), but his visit had met with no success. Paul himself paid an unhappy visit to Corinth (2 Cor. 2:1) and wrote a severe letter (2 Cor. 2:3; 7:8-12). In response to his critics, Paul in 2 Corinthians finds it necessary to defend his conduct and his apostleship and offers an extended defense of his ministry (2:14—7:3). Whereas he barely mentions the need for the Corinthians to participate in the collection in 1 Corinthians, he devotes the entirety of chapters 8 and 9 in 2 Corinthians to encourage them to participate in that effort. Chapters 10—13 contain a defense of his apostleship and a strong indication that the opponents were about to undermine everything he had sought to do there.

The change of subject matter in 2 Corinthians makes it apparent that Paul wrote the book only after that church had experienced considerable tensions. The situation in the Corinthian church can best be ascertained when we reconstruct the events leading up to the writing of 2 Corinthians. Several statements of Paul in the two epistles, in addition to information from Acts, lead to this reconstruction.

1. Paul arrives at Corinth from Athens (A.D. 50) and establishes the church there. He stays with Aquila and Priscilla (Acts 18).
2. Paul leaves Corinth after 18 months (A.D. 52), leaving Aquila and Priscilla at Ephesus and going to Caesarea and Antioch.
3. Paul goes to Ephesus and makes this city his center of activity for probably three years (A.D. 52-55).
4. Paul writes a letter to Corinth concerning immorality in the church there (1 Cor. 5:9). This letter was written prior to our 1 Corinthians, probably in A.D. 52 or 53.
5. The Corinthians write Paul a letter asking certain questions about marital relations, idol foods, order in worship, etc. (see above). Paul responds with our 1 Corinthians (fall of A.D. 54 or spring of 55).
6. Timothy is sent to Corinth, perhaps carrying 1 Corinthians (1 Cor. 16:10, 11). Around this time, before Timothy arrived, false apostles came to Corinth in an attempt to undermine Paul's work. They suceeded in gaining a large following.
7. Timothy returns to Paul in Ephesus with a bad report of the conditions at Corinth. Paul hastens by ship to Corinth, but his visit is "painful" and unsuccessful (cf. 2:1). He returns to Ephesus.
8. Paul, having told the Corinthians he would go back to Corinth before going to Macedonia, writes a letter in lieu of that visit. This letter was writ-

ten "with many tears," "out of much affliction and anguish of heart" (2:4). This letter was carried to Corinth by Titus.

9. After the riot in Ephesus (Acts 19:23ff.), Paul leaves Ephesus for Troas (spring, A.D. 55). He had arranged with Titus to meet him along a pre-arranged route. Paul hoped to see Titus at Troas, but did not find him there (2 Cor. 2:12, 13). Not finding Titus, Paul went on to Macedonia.

10. Somewhere in Macedonia, Titus returns to Paul with the report that the situation in Corinth is improved. Paul, along with Timothy, sends a letter (our 2 Corinthians) which is taken by Titus and two brothers. They are to gather the Corinthian collection before Paul himself arrives in Corinth (2 Cor. 8:16-23; 9:4). Paul was planning a visit shortly (2 Cor. 12:14; 13:1).

The immediate background of 2 Corinthians is the information Paul had received from Titus. Titus had brought good news to Paul. The Corinthians had had a change of heart. On Paul's "painful visit" (2:1), he had been confronted with open rebellion, led particularly by one who seems to have been very offensive to Paul (2:5ff.). Now Titus reported to Paul that the Corinthians had repented; they had inflicted punishment on the one who had personally offended Paul (7:11, 15). They had been "grieved into repenting" and had proved themselves "at every point . . . guiltless in the matter" (7:8-11). Because of the Corinthians' change of heart, there is a note of joy in the book. "But God, who comforts the downcast, comforted me with the coming of Titus" (7:6).

Now that the crisis is over, Paul writes the church from Macedonia to express his relief at the good news which Titus has brought of the improved attitude of the Corinthians toward Paul. This fact is particularly clear in chapter 7. Yet because of the criticisms that had been leveled against Paul, he found it necessary to make several explanations. He had to explain his change of travel plans, since he had been charged with fickleness (1:15ff.).

He found it necessary to encourage the church to be more sympathetic toward the offender whom they had disciplined (2:5ff.). Although Paul was pleased over their progress, the dangers are not completely averted. Paul's explanations show that the influence of the false teachers is still felt. Because of the influence of his opponents, Paul defends himself throughout the book; indeed he continues to warn the Corinthians about their influence, still fearing that the Corinthians could yield to them again (see 13:2).

The Opponents

We have already observed that Paul met bitter opposition on his second trip to Corinth. This conflict was no mere continuation of the strife which 1 Corinthians condemns. Certain Jewish Christians (11:22) had arrived in Corinth, carrying letters of recommendation (3:1) and claiming the right to exercise authoritative leadership in the churches (11:5). In all probability they came with the deliberate purpose of undermining the influence of Paul. In this they succeeded.

One of the main points in the accusations that the opponents made was that Paul had no right to call himself an apostle (12:12; 3:2ff.). In person he made a remarkably uncertain impression. His letters were very forceful, but his bodily presence was weak (10:1, 9). In eloquence and other qualities necessary for a missionary, he left much to be desired (11:5f). He was a schemer, and his conduct aroused suspicion (1:12ff.; 3:12f.; 4:1f.; 5:11). By refusing support from the churches he betrayed a lack of love for the church at Corinth (11:7-12; 12:13). He changed his plans capriciously, without thinking of his promises to the church (1:15ff.). In fact, they accused him of outright dishonesty, implying that the collection for the saints at Jerusalem, to which Paul gave so much attention, enriched himself and not the churches.

Although Paul engages in strong debate with his opponents, he tells surprisingly little about the doctrines

11

they espoused. We know from 11:22 that they were Jews. They took considerable pride in their Jewish descent, claiming also to be "Hebrews," and "of the seed of Abraham." Some have inferred that Paul's opponents must have been Judaizers like those which we find in Galatians. However, there is no indication from 2 Corinthians that Paul is debating a Judaizing tendency. Certainly he does not enter into the kind of impassioned polemic in 2 Corinthians which we find in Galatians. Nowhere in 2 Corinthians does Paul argue about circumcision; there is no attention given to the question of "salvation by works." Therefore, Paul is faced in 2 Corinthians with a different problem from that which he faced in Galatians.

Some have found traces of a polemic against a kind of Gnosticism in 2 Corinthians. Certainly Paul polemicizes against elements in this ancient heresy in such later epistles as Colossians and Ephesians. Possibly Paul's polemic against the abuse of Christian freedom in 1 Corinthians is an argument against a form of Gnosticism. However, in 2 Corinthians it is difficult to find any doctrinal position that we can label. The argument in 2 Corinthians centers basically around the legitimacy of Paul's apostleship.

The book of 2 Corinthians is one side of an argument between Paul and his Jewish opponents. We may ascertain from a number of Paul's statements the following features of the teaching of his opponents.

1. They claimed to be "apostles of Christ" (11:5, 13) and "servants of Christ" (11:23). But their view of apostleship was different from Paul's. Paul's model for an apostle was none other than his Lord. Thus Paul imitates the Lord in accepting suffering for himself (6:3ff.; 4:10, 11). He imitates the "meekness and gentleness of Christ" (10:1). What for Paul was a sign of his apostleship was for his opponents a sign of his weakness (10:10). They modeled themselves after a different idea of apostleship: they boasted of their Jewish descent (11:22), their gift of speech (10:10), and their miraculous signs (12:9).

2. They proclaimed "another Jesus" (11:4). Whereas

Paul proclaimed the suffering and death of Christ (4:10, 11; 5:16ff.), they were interested in the human Jesus. They claim to know Jesus from a "human point of view." They were interested in Jesus as a wonder-worker and teacher and not in his cross. Thus, they modeled themselves after their view of Jesus.

3. They boasted of their "ecstasy" or spiritual experiences (5:13; 12:1-8). The signs of a true apostle were his miraculous powers (12:9). They accused Paul of not having spiritual gifts, of acting like a "worldly man" (1:17) when he made his decisions. Their interest in eloquence probably indicates that they were especially concerned with speech as a spiritual gift (cf. 11:6). Paul did not deny the validity of such spiritual experiences, but they were not for him criteria for judging one's apostleship.

4. They took pay for their work (11:20). They followed the normal custom of itinerant preachers in demanding support. Furthermore, they accused Paul of great injustice in not accepting support.

5. They appear to have had a special interest in Moses. Paul's argument in 2 Corinthians 3:7-18 indicates that they were exalting Moses. It is probable that they thought of themselves as "servants of Moses," since Paul finds it necessary to show that his ministry is superior to the ministry of Moses.

LITERARY QUESTIONS

Because transitions in 2 Corinthians are often abrupt, the literary unity of 2 Corinthians has often been questioned. Two literary questions in particular have been the subject of much discussion.

1. One may notice in 2 Corinthians 6:14—7:1 an exhortation that appears to be an extraneous insertion into Paul's personal address to the congregation. The subject of Paul's reconciliation to the congregation is interrupted with the admonition to have no connections with unbelievers. Furthermore, one may notice that if 6:14—7:1 is

omitted, 6:13 ("widen your hearts also") connects with 7:2 ("open your hearts to us").

Since 6:14—7:1 appears to break the thought pattern here, it has been thought by many scholars not to be an original part of the text. Additionally, since the subject of 6:14—7:1 is the same issue as that which Paul confronts in the "previous letter" alluded to in 1 Corinthians 5:9, it is an attractive hypothesis that 6:14—7:1 is really a section from Paul's original letter to the Corinthians However, one must not forget in this case that it was not at all unusual for Paul to digress from one subject to another without transition. Furthermore, if we understand the "unbelievers" to be Paul's opponents at 6:14, this unit (6:14—7:1) fits very well here. Paul is discussing the need for reconciliation between himself and the church there (6:13; 7:2). Before reconciliation can take place, the "unbelievers," that is, Paul's opponents, must be expelled (7:1). Thus the section 6:14—7:1 would not be out of place here.

2. A more important question centers around the relation of chapters 10—13 to the rest of the epistle. Whereas in chapters 1—7 Paul speaks with joy of the fact that he and the Corinthians have made up their quarrel, in chapters 10—13 Paul vigorously attacks his opponents who are undermining his work. Thus one gets a much different view of Paul's relationship to the church from chapters 10—13 than he gets from chapters 1—9.

Several explanatory views have been offered; two in particular deserve some comment. One is the view that Paul, after writing chapters 1—9, recieved more news of the opponents at Corinth, causing him to write the final chapters with considerable bitterness. Probably the view most widely held is that chapters 10—13 were written before chapters 1—9. According to this view, chapters 10—13 are at least part of the intermediate letter which Paul mentions in 2 Corinthians 2:4: the letter written "out of much anguish and tears." Either of these views has much to commend it.

Both of the above views assume that chapters 1—9 and 10—13 speak to such different situations that they could not have been written at the same time. Although the differences are great, they are not necessarily such that Paul could not have written them at the same time. It must not be overlooked that although Paul is happy with the Corinthians' progress in 1—9, he still is aware of the presence of his critics. Consequently, he continues to offer defenses for his conduct (1:13ff.; 4:2f.; 5:11f.). Furthermore, it is very conceivable that some time elapsed between the writing of 1—9 and 10—13. There is no reason to assume here that Paul must have written such a long letter at one sitting. Finally, there is another view that deserves attention. The change of tone is explained by the assumption that while chapters 1—9 are addressed to faithful Christians, chapters 10—13 are addressed to Paul's opponents.

The best supposition appears to be that 2 Corinthians, though it contains abrupt transitions, was first transmitted as a unity in its present form. Anyone who attempts to partition the book must explain how this process took place. All manuscript evidence points to the conclusion that 2 Corinthians was first transmitted in its present form. If it is a composite of two letters, then we must assume that at a very early date someone pieced two letters together. Furthermore, we would have to assume that the end of one letter and the beginning of another were lost, making the two parts fit together. Therefore, any view that 2 Corinthians is a composite of two letters is suspect. Although 2 Corinthians shows a change of tone at chapter 10, this is not enough reason to assume that we are dealing with two separate letters. Paul dictated his letters in the midst of interruptions, and thus the existence of abrupt changes of subject matter is not very surprising.

PLACE AND DATE OF COMPOSITION

Between the composition of 1 Corinthians and 2 Corinthians, the following events took place: the return of Timothy from Corinth, the journey of Paul to Corinth, his return to Ephesus, the sending of Titus to Corinth, the beginning and breaking off of Paul's missionary activity in Troas, his journey to Macedonia, and his meeting there with Titus. According to Acts 20:2-16, Paul made another visit to Corinth soon after the writing of 2 Corinthians.

All of these events can be fitted within a six-month period of time. Thus, if 1 Corinthians was written in the spring of 54 or 55, 2 Corinthians was written late that year.

One difficulty to this dating is Paul's statement that the collection was commenced "a year ago." This statement would refer to Paul's mentioning of the collection at 1 Corinthians 16:1. Does the phrase "a year ago" indicate that at least a year elapsed between the composition of the two Corinthian epistles? Since the Macedonian New Year began on September 21, the most likely explanation of "a year ago" is that a new year had begun between the composition of the two epistles. Thus, late 54 or 55 is the most likely date for the epistle. Since it was in Macedonia that Paul met Titus, the epistle must have been written from Macedonia.

Importance of 2 Corinthians

Two factors make 2 Corinthians a very important book for understanding the life of the earliest church. In the first place, 2 Corinthians is one of the most autobiographical of Paul's epistles. From chapter 11 one learns of the great trials Paul experienced which are unrecorded in Acts. There is also the fact that while Luke may chronicle Paul's journeys in Acts, only Paul can tell of his personal "anxiety for the churches" and his joy at their repentance. In the same way, only Paul can describe his "thorn in the flesh" (2 Cor. 12:7-10).

The second factor which makes the epistle important is that 2 Corinthians describes more fully than any other epistle Paul's conception of his ministry. The claims to authority made by Paul's opponents and their charges against him have caused Paul to describe what the Christian ministry is (chapters 3—5). It is a ministry of the Spirit, a ministry of the new covenant (3:6), and a ministry of reconciliation (5:18). It is marked, not by cunning, but by the acceptance of the cross of Christ by the Christian minister (4:7-12).

OUTLINE OF CONTENTS

INTRODUCTION

BIBLIOGRAPHY

DAVIES, W. D. *Paul and Rabbinic Judaism*. London: SPCK, 1948.

FILSON, FLOYD. "The Second Epistle to the Corinthians," *The Interpreter's Bible*, Vol. 10. New York: Abingdon, 1953.

FRIEDRICH, G. "Die Gegner des Paulus im 2 Korintherbrief," *Abraham unser Vater*, ed. O. Betz, M. Hengel, P. Schmidt. Leiden: E. J. Brill, 1963.

GÄRTNER, B. *The Temple and the Community in Qumran and the New Testament*. Cambridge: University Press, 1965.

GEORGI, D. *Die Gegner des Paulus im 2 Korintherbrief*. Neukirchener-Vluyn: Neukirchener Verlag, 1964.

HÉRING, JEAN. *The Second Epistle of Saint Paul to the Corinthians*. London: Epworth Press, 1967.

HURD, JOHN C. *The Origin of I Corinthians*. London: SPCK, 1965.

KÜMMEL, W. G. *Introduction to the New Testament*. New York: Abingdon, 1966.

LIETZMANN, H. *An die Korinther I, II*. Tübingen: J.C.B. Mohr, 1949.

MARXSEN, W. *Introduction to the New Testament*. Philadelphia: Fortress Press, 1968.

MUNCK, JOHANNES. *Paul and the Salvation of Mankind*. Richmond: John Knox Press, 1959.

PLUMMER, ALFRED. *A Critical and Exegetical Commentary on the Second Epistle of St. Paul to the Corinthians*. International Critical Commentary. Edinburgh: T&T Clark, 1915.

SCHMITHALS, W. *Die Gnosis in Korinth*. Göttingen: Vandenhoeck and Ruprecht, 1965.

STRACHAN, R. H. *The Second Epistle of Paul to the Corinthians*. New York: Harper and Row, 1935.

The Second Letter of Paul
to the Corinthians

INTRODUCTION, 1:1-11

Salutation, 1:1, 2

ANCIENT LETTERS normally began with an introductory
paragraph containing the name of the writer, the name
of the recipient, and a greeting. Paul used the customary
form in all of his epistles. Generally, he followed the
practice of dictating his letters to an amanuensis (see
Rom. 16:22).

[1] Paul identifies himself as **an apostle of Jesus Christ
through the will of God.** It was Paul's custom to write
with authority, expecting obedience from the recipients
of the letter. By describing himself as **an apostle,** Paul
places himself in a position of authority (cf. Rom. 1:1;
1 Cor. 1:1; Gal. 1:1). The word **apostle,** meaning literally
"one who is sent," is not used in a uniform sense in the
New Testament (cf. vol. 10, pp. 34f. and vol. 13, pp. 43f.).
In the Gospels the word is exclusively applied to the
twelve whom Jesus appointed (Matt. 10:2; Mark 3:14;
Luke 6:13). In Acts and in the epistles, the word is applied to others (Acts 14:4, 14; Gal. 1:19). In 1 Corinthians 9:1, Paul says that the criterion for a true apostle

19

¹ **Paul, an apostle of Christ Jesus by the will of God, and Timothy our brother.**

To the church of God which is at Corinth, with all the saints who are in the whole of Achaia:

---

is that he must have been an eyewitness to the resurrected Lord (cf. Acts 1:21f.). For other meanings, see 2 Corinthians 8:23 and 11:5.

Paul ascribes his position to **the will of God.** This expression, used also at 1 Corinthians 1:1, is more than an assertion of God's general control of events; it is a claim that Paul's apostleship rests on a direct intervention by God on the Damascus road. Indeed, Paul goes further in Galatians 1:15 to say that God chose him before he was born, thus comparing his call to Jeremiah's (cf. Jer. 1:5; Isa. 49:5). Against the "pseudo-apostles" (11:3) who have attempted to undermine his authority, Paul claims an appointment by the will of God.

Paul is joined in the writing of the epistle by **Timothy our brother.** According to Acts 16:1, Timothy began accompanying Paul at Lystra on the second missionary journey. His relationship to the Corinthian church is indicated at 1 Corinthians 4:17 and 16:10. Paul intended to send Timothy to Corinth on an important mission, but the results are never recorded. Timothy is called **our brother.** Although the word "apostle" is applied to such people as Barnabas and James (the Lord's brother), it is never applied to Timothy. More than once, Paul describes him simply as a "brother" (Col. 1:1; Phil. 1:1).

The letter is addressed **to the church of God,** including **all the saints who are in the whole of Achaia.** Here **Achaia** means the province of which Corinth was the center; Christians at Cenchrea (Rom. 16:1) and Athens would be included. Mention of the region of Achaia indicates that this letter had an audience wider than one church (cf. 1 Cor. 1:2; Gal. 1:2; Col. 4:16). Although Paul's letters had primary reference to a specific church, they were of value to other churches also. **Church** and **saints** are here parallel expressions. One may compare 1 Corinthians

² Grace to you and peace from God our Father and the Lord Jesus Christ.

³ Blessed be the God and Father of our Lord Jesus Christ, the Father of mercies and God of all comfort,

---

1:2, where the church is identified with "those sanctified in Christ Jesus" and "called to be saints." The word "saint" (*hagios*) in the New Testament carries the idea of one who has been sanctified by the Spirit (2 Thess. 2:13f.; 1 Peter 1:2), who has been set apart for God's purpose, and who has accepted the demand to imitate God's holiness (1 Peter 1:15f.).

[2] The formula **grace** and **peace** is found at the beginning of all the Pauline epistles (1 and 2 Timothy add "mercy"). This greeting unites in one a modification of the Greek salutation (*chaire*, "hail!" to *charis*, "grace") and the Hebrew (*shalom*, "peace"). Both words have a religious significance in the Christian faith, as the end of the verse indicates. Salvation comes by grace (Eph. 2:8), and the result of this grace is "peace with God" (Rom. 5:1).

Thanksgiving for Recent Deliverance, 1:3-11

[3] Except for Galatians, where the situation called for sharp rebuke, Paul's letters follow the widespread custom of adding an expression of thanksgiving to the address and greeting. In the other letters he frequently thanks God for the faith, hope and love of the readers (e.g., 1 Thess. 1:3), but here he offers thanks to God for the **comfort** given him. Only here and at Ephesians 1:3 does Paul use the characteristic Jewish expression, **blessed be God** (*eulogētos ho theos*). *Eulogētos* is used exclusively of God in the New Testament, always as a doxology (Luke 1:68; Rom. 1:25; 9:5; 2 Cor. 11:31). The expression probably reflects an often used formula in the synagogue and church (cf. 1 Peter 1:3).

God is **Father of our Lord Jesus Christ** (cf. Eph. 1:3). Although Paul affirmed the equality of Christ to God (Phil. 2:6), he also affirmed a subordination of Christ to God (cf. 1 Cor. 15:24). For Paul, Christ is God's son in

⁴ who comforts us in all our affliction, so that we may
be able to comfort those who are in any affliction, with
the comfort with which we ourselves are comforted by
God. ⁵ For as we share abundantly in Christ's sufferings, so
through Christ we share abundantly in comfort too.ᵃ

ᵃ Or, *For as the sufferings of Christ abound for us, so also our comfort
abounds through Christ*

---

a unique way, having been declared son by the resurrection (Rom. 1:4). It is through Christ that the Christian
is able to say "Abba, father" (Gal. 4:6).

The key word in verses 3-11 is **comfort,** which as a
verb or noun is used ten times. Thus God is described
here as **father of mercies** (*oiktirmos*) and **God of all comfort** (*paraklēsis*). Paul frequently hints at the contents
of his letters within the introduction to the epistle. His
reference to comfort here in the introduction points forward to an important theme in the epistle (cf. 2:7; 7:6,
13). **Mercy** (*oiktirmos*) is attributed to God in the Old
Testament (Ex. 33:19). Indeed, he is the source of all
mercy. Thus Paul says, "I appeal to you by the mercies
of God" (Rom. 12:1). It is a quality that is also a Christian virtue (Phil. 2:1). **Comfort** also has its source in
God (Isa. 51:3). The ancient prophet was commissioned
with the message, "Comfort, comfort, my people" (Isa.
40:1). The Messiah was expected to bring **comfort** to his
people (Isa. 61:2).

[4] The function of Paul's description of God is made
clear at verses 4-11. Paul has experienced a severe crisis,
but he is able to say that God is the one who **comforts**
(*parakalōn*) us in every **affliction** (*thlipsis*). Only in
verse 8 does Paul mention any specific affliction. Yet he
is very concerned with afflictions throughout 2 Corinthians (4:8; 7:4, 5).

[5] For Paul, **affliction** and suffering are necessary
aspects of the Christian life. The Christian actually shares
in Christ's sufferings (1:5) and completes "what is lacking
in Christ's afflictions for the sake of his body, that is, the
church" (Col. 3:24). Jewish literature, including rab-

⁶ If we are afflicted, it is for your comfort and salvation;
and if we are comforted, it is for your comfort, which you
experience when you patiently endure the same sufferings
that we suffer. ⁷ Our hope for you is unshaken; for we know
that as you share in our sufferings, you will also share in our
comfort.

---

binical and apocryphal texts, often taught that before the
dawn of the Messianic kingdom, the people must pass
through an age of mounting affliction. This period, according to Paul, began with the suffering of Jesus. It
continues in the sufferings of his disciples.

The literal reading of the Greek is, "the sufferings of
Christ overflow to us." Paul conceived of a "fellowship of
his sufferings" (Phil. 3:10), an expression which is also
found at 1 Peter 4:13. **Christ's sufferings** here refer to the
suffering which Jesus experienced in the flesh. But although Jesus' sufferings are unique, it remains for the
disciple to drink his cup and be baptized with his baptism (Mark 10:39). This fellowship or "sharing" in Christ's
sufferings takes place when the disciple reenacts the sufferings of Christ. The cross of suffering is at the center
of the Christian faith, and each disciple must take his
own cross (Mark 8:31). Although Jesus' sufferings were
unique because he was unique, his disciples find it necessary to share this experience. Jesus warned that his fate
would be reproduced by his disciples: "If they persecuted
me, they will persecute you" (John 15:20). The **share** in
his **comfort** is realized when the disciple realizes that his
suffering is not meaningless, that indeed he is following
the path of his Lord; and the path of suffering experienced
by Jesus ended in triumph. Thus there is comfort through
suffering.

[6, 7] Paul thinks of the positive effects of his suffering. After the alienation which separated him from the
Corinthians, he attempts to bring about reconciliation by
recalling their common experience of affliction. Paul's affliction was for the benefit of the Corinthians. His affliction results in their **salvation** (*sōteria*). He is not speak-

⁸ For we do not want you to be ignorant, brethren, of the affliction we experienced in Asia; for we were so utterly, unbearably crushed that we despaired of life itself. ⁹ Why, we felt that we had received the sentence of death; but that was to make us rely not on ourselves but on God who raises the dead; ¹⁰ he delivered us from so deadly a peril, and he will deliver us; on him we have set our hope that he will deliver us again.

---

ing of a substitute salvation that he is able to effect. He thinks, rather, of the positive results of suffering. Suffering produces endurance (Rom. 5:3). Despite recent wavering, Paul's **hope** is unshaken. There is one condition to this hope, however: the acceptance of suffering.

[8] Following the general praise of God for help and comfort (1:3-7), Paul recalls a specific instance of suffering. Apparently the Corinthians knew of Paul's recent deliverance from death, since Paul gives no details. The expression, **we do not want you to be ignorant,** is a favorite way for Paul to emphasize his point (cf. Rom. 1:13; 1 Cor. 10:1; 12:1). The affliction occurred in Asia, the Roman province in western Asia Minor. Ephesus was the chief city, and thus the event may have happened there. Some have seen the clue in 1 Corinthians 15:32, "I fought with wild beasts at Ephesus." That event, regardless of whether the language was literal or not, was probably too long in the past to be fresh on Paul's mind here. Perhaps Paul has in mind the riot in Ephesus which occurred just prior to the time Paul left that city (Acts 19:23; 20:1). If he is not referring to that event, then we must conclude that the occasion Paul refers to here is, like the events of 2 Corinthians 11:23-26, unrecorded elsewhere.

[9, 10] Here, as in verse 4, Paul sees a divine purpose in his suffering. God was teaching him to **rely** not on himself (cf. 4:7; 12:9), but on God. Paul knew a prayer from the synagogue, known as the Eighteen Benedictions, which described God as the one **who raises the dead** (cf. 4:14; Rom. 4:17). Paul knew that because God delivered Jesus Christ from death, he will **deliver us** (see Job 33:30). Hope

¹¹ You also must help us by prayer, so that many will give thanks on our behalf for the blessing granted us in answer to many prayers.

¹² For our boast is this, the testimony of our conscience that we have behaved in the world, and still more toward you, with holiness and godly sincerity, not by earthly wisdom, but by the grace of God.

---

is here grounded, not on wishful thinking, but on God's past performance. God confirmed at the resurrection, and in Paul's recent deliverance, that he could be trusted.

[11] Just as faith and God's goodness lead Paul to hope, so the faith and gratitude of the Corinthians must find expression in intercessory **prayer** (cf. Rom. 15:30; Eph. 6:18; Col. 4:3; 1 Thess. 5:25). Paul believes that God will help him; but through prayer the Corinthians must share in Paul's support, to the end that God will give Paul a **blessing** (his preservation), and that **many will give thanks** to God for his goodness to Paul. The result of their prayers will thus be the edification of the church.

PAUL'S MINISTRY, 1:12—7:16

His Plans, 1:12—2:17

The Charge of Fickleness, 1:12-23. [12] Beginning at verse 12 and continuing through chapter 2, Paul answers the charges which have been made against him by the Corinthian church and the "pseudo-apostles" (11:13) there. Paul begins his defense, **For our boast is this.** The word **boast** (*kauchēsis*) is generally used by Paul with a bad connotation, indicating the boastful pride of those who depend on themselves and not on God (see Rom. 3:21-26). When he does boast, he realizes that his boasting is grounded in what God has done through him. We notice at 11:17, 18 that the boasting of Paul's enemies has caused him to boast in self-defense.

Paul's boast is that he acted with integrity: **with holiness and Godly sincerity.** Some manuscripts, instead of **holiness,**

25

¹³ **For we write you nothing but what you can read and
understand; I hope you will understand fully,** ¹⁴ **as you have
understood in part, that you can be proud of us as we can
be of you, on the day of the Lord Jesus.**
  ¹⁵ **Because I was sure of this, I wanted to come to you
first, so that you might have a double pleasure;** ^b ¹⁶ **I wanted**
    ^b Other ancient authorities read *favor*

---

have the word which means "singleness of purpose." **Holiness** is better attested by manuscript tradition. His point is
that he has always acted with moral purity, and thus he has
nothing to be ashamed of.

Paul contrasts his behavior to that of his opponents:
not by earthly wisdom. In 1 Corinthians Paul consistently
denigrates human wisdom, setting it in contrast to the
power of the cross (1 Cor. 1:17ff.) and the higher, heavenly
wisdom (3:19). Here Paul's point is that his change of
plans did not come from worldly motives (see 1:17).

[13a] Paul's integrity is also in question with regard to
his letters. Continually in 2 Corinthians he has to answer
the charge of deception (3:13; 2:17; 7:2; 10:9-11). Moffatt's paraphrase is apt here: "You don't have to read between the lines of my letters." He is not evasive; he is
clear and direct in what he says.

[13b, 14] Paul hopes that the Corinthian church will
comprehend his intentions. At present they know only in
part. Living in the present age, we are limited in knowledge; "we know in part" (1 Cor. 13:12). Even though Paul
writes clearly, the Corinthians still know in part, even
about his affairs. When Christ returns, we will cease to know
in part; then we will understand fully (1 Cor. 13:10-12).
When the Corinthians come to this point, they will be
proud of Paul, as Paul is proud of them.

The literal expression is, "we are your boast and you
are our boast." Paul often expresses the hope that his
churches will be his boast at the second coming of the
Lord (1 Thess. 2:19f.; Phil. 2:16). Now his hope is that
they will understand that he is their boast. They must thank
God that he has given them Paul (1:11; 5:12).

to visit you on my way to Macedonia, and to come back
to you from Macedonia and have you send me on my way
to Judea. ¹⁷ Was I vacillating when I wanted to do this?
Do I make my plans like a worldly man, ready to say Yes
and No at once?

[15, 16] Because Paul has changed his travel plans, he
has been accused to being unreliable. In 1 Corinthians
16:5-9 Paul had announced his plans of coming to Corinth
(see Acts 19:21) to spend some time with them. Again,
during his short "painful visit" to Corinth (see 2:1), he
made a promise that he would go to Corinth first (*proteron*)
before going to Macedonia, his destination. He could then
come back through Corinth, thus giving them a double
pleasure (*deuteran charan*, "second joy"), or, as other
manuscripts indicate, "a double favor" (*deuteran charin*).
The latter reading has slightly better support among the
best manuscripts.

Paul had wanted to have the Corinthians send him to
Judea. The word used here for **send** (*propempein*) is a
technical term for the support of a missionary (see 1 Cor.
16:6, 11, where the same word is used). To send (*propempein*) a missionary was to provide him with food,
money, and means of travel. This trip to Judea, in which
Paul is to deliver the collection for the saints there (8:4;
cf. Rom. 15:25), has not yet taken place (see chapters 8—
9). Paul's failure to carry out his plan here may have
caused his critics to accuse him of "overextending" himself
(see 10:14), and of lack of concern for them (11:7-11).
Paul's real reason for delaying his visit is that he wanted
to wait for a more opportune time.

[17] Two charges have been made against Paul: (1)
that he is fickle, and (2) that he makes his **plans like a
worldly man** (*kata sarka*, "according to the flesh"), thus
not listening to the guidance of the Spirit. This charge is
mentioned again at 10:2. Paul responds at 10:3 that he is
not fighting a worldly war. He lives, instead, by divine
power. According to Paul's opponents, the result of Paul's
behavior was that he said **Yes** and **No** at once; or rather,

27

¹⁸ As surely as God is faithful, our word to you has **not** been Yes and No. ¹⁹ For the Son of God, Jesus Christ, whom we preached among you, Silvanus, Timothy, and I, was not Yes and No; but in him it is always Yes. ²⁰ For all the promises of God find their Yes in him. That is why we utter the Amen through him, to the glory of God. ²¹ But it is God who establishes us with you in Christ, and has com-missioned us; ²² he has put his seal upon us and given us his Spirit in our hearts as a guarantee.

---

that his **Yes** was quickly and arbitrarily changed to a **No** at the slightest whim.

[18] When Paul wants to give support to a claim, he often appeals to God as guarantor. Thus he here uses the common expression, **God is faithful** (God is trustworthy; cf. 1 Cor. 1:9; 10:13). God is Paul's guarantor that Paul did not change his plans at the slightest whim.

[19] Paul also appeals to Jesus Christ and to the mes-sage he preaches to defend his behavior. Christ is himself God's **Yes**, i.e., the guarantee that God keeps his promise. Christ, is, according to Revelation 3:14, the "Amen."

[20] The Corinthians cannot dispute that Christ is God's **Yes** to his promise; they affirm in their public wor-ship that Christ is the fulfillment of God's promise by saying the **Amen** (1 Cor. 14:16). Paul's message cannot be separated from his conduct (1 Thess. 1:4, 5). Therefore, Paul's conduct is not Yes and No (vs. 18). His conduct, like his message is an unequivocal Yes. His conduct has made it clear that he, like God, stands behind his word.

[21, 22] Verses 21 and 22 state the relationship of the church to God, Christ, and the Holy Spirit. This relation-ship has made Jesus the one to whom they say the Amen. Paul never gives a detailed theological discussion of the Trinity (see 2 Cor. 13:14). He is content to show here that they are united in the redemptive work.

Paul uses four participles to describe the divine activity in redemption. Paul reminds them of the redemption which he, by his ministry, has made available to them. By re-minding them of their hope and of their experience of the

²³ But I call God to witness against me—it was to spare
you that I refrained from coming to Corinth.

Holy Spirit, he hopes to prove to them that his motives
have always been pure. God **establishes** (*ho bebaiōn*). The
Greek word *bebaios* was a legal word for a binding
guarantee of a sale. Thus Paul thinks in the legal sphere to
say that God has made his guarantee. Secondly, Paul
says that God is the one who has **commissioned us**
(*chrisas*). The word for "commission" is literally the
word for "anoint." Thus the word Christ means "anointed
one." Only here and at 1 John 2:20, 27 is it said that Christians are anointed. In the Old Testament, anointing was a
ceremony whereby kings and priests were commissioned
for a service. In the New Testament, the Christian is
anointed when he receives the Holy Spirit at baptism. This
act is his commission.

In verse 22 Paul says that God is the one who has
sealed us (*sphragisamenos hēmas*). In the Old Testament,
Abraham received circumcision as a seal of his relation to
God (Rom. 4:11; Gen. 17:10f.). In the New Testament,
the Holy Spirit is one's seal (Eph. 4:30; 1:13; cf. Rev.
7:3; 9:4; 14:1). Very likely, Paul thinks here of the act of
baptism, in which one becomes sealed with the Holy Spirit.

Paul further says that God has **given us his Spirit in
our hearts as a guarantee.** The **Spirit,** according to Paul, is
the possession of all believers (cf. Rom. 8:11, 15, 16, 26).
In this passage, the Spirit is called a **guarantee** (*arrabōna*).
That the Spirit is a guarantee is affirmed at 5:5 and in
Ephesians 1:14. An *arrabōn,* or **guarantee,** is, like the word
bebaios above, a legal word. It is a "deposit," or first installment, a pledge that full payment will be made. The
word is often used in the sense of "earnest money" ratifying
a contract. Thus the Holy Spirit, in which Christians were
sealed at baptism, is God's "down payment" or pledge of
future redemption. Indeed, according to Romans 8:11, it
is only through the indwelling of the Holy Spirit that the
Christian will be resurrected.

[23] Paul now reveals the true motive for his travel

²⁴ Not that we lord it over your faith; we work with you for your joy, for you stand firm in your faith.

¹ For I made up my mind not to make you another painful visit.

---

plans. To add force to his statement, Paul calls God as **witness,** an oath which Paul uses frequently (Rom. 1:9; Phil. 1:8; 1 Thess. 2:15). To add additional force, Paul not only calls God as witness but pledges his very self. The expression **against me** (*epi tēn emēn psuchēn*) is a conditional curse which Paul pronounces upon himself. One can see how important it was for Paul to reestablish confidence with the Corinthian church.

Paul chose not to come in order to **spare** them. As early as 1 Corinthians 4:18-21, Paul was threatening to visit them in order to exercise discipline. Even then many were saying that Paul would not come. Many of Paul's opponents seem to have accused Paul of being so weak that he would not exercise apostolic discipline (see 10:10). Here and at 13:10, Paul assures his readers that, as a last resort, he can exercise his authority in a very stern way.

[24] Because the word "spare" in verse 23 might sound domineering, Paul here adds the expression, **not that we lord it over your faith.** Faith cannot be coerced. The Christian leader is told in 1 Peter 5:3 that he is not to "lord it over" his followers. Paul is no despot in matters of faith; he is a servant who tries to help his congregations understand what their discipleship means.

The Reason for His Delay, 2:1-17. The connection with what precedes is very close. At 1:24, Paul has shown what he did not mean when he spoke of sparing them. Now he explains what he does mean.

[1] Paul's use of the verb *ekrina* (**I made up my mind**) excludes any thought of levity or caprice in his decision making (cf. Rom. 14:13; 2 Cor. 5:14, where the same verb is used). Paul mentions here a visit that is unrecorded in Acts. According to Acts, Paul stayed in Corinth for a year and a half on his first visit (Acts 18:1-18), and no "grief" was involved. This second, **painful** visit is also re-

² For if I cause you pain, who is there to make me glad but
the one whom I have pained? ³ And I wrote as I did, so
that when I came I might not be pained by those who
should have made me rejoice, for I felt sure of all of you,
that my joy would be the joy of you all.

---

flected in 12:14 and 13:1, 2. At that time, he had promised
to return soon before going to Macedonia. But later he
decided to delay his return. Not wanting to make another
"painful visit," he sent Titus with the stern letter. Paul
himself waited for news from Titus before acting further
with the Corinthian church.

[2] Paul's life was so intimately involved with his
churches that their sorrow was his sorrow. Consequently,
he would have no sadistic pleasure in causing more pain
to them; such pain Paul would have shared. In the same
way, their joy is also his joy. It is very doubtful whether
the one who is **to make me glad** or the one **I have pained**
are specific persons. Paul's point is that he cannot bring
himself to cause further pain to his only source of joy. Any
severity on the part of Paul, such as that which he threatens
at 12:21 and 13:2, will come only as a last resort.

[3] Paul's grief was also communicated by letter. Literally, Paul says, I wrote *this very thing*, i.e., that to spare
them he was delaying his visit (see 13:10). Although the
letter caused pain in writing (vs. 4) and to those who received it (7:8, 9), it was to be preferred over an unhappy
meeting. His purpose in writing was to provoke them to
repentance, and Paul wrote with the confidence that the
result would be good (7:14).

Paul's allusion to this previous letter (see 7:12) leaves
two possibilities: (1) either the letter was lost or, (2) it
is contained, as the majority of scholarly opinion holds, in
chapters 10—13 of 2 Corinthians. That he is not referring
to 1 Corinthians is apparent from Paul's description of the
letter. There is no evidence that 1 Corinthians was written
in grief or that its purpose was to "spare" the readers. If
chapters 10—13 are from this "painful" letter, it represents
only a portion, since (1) these chapters make no mention

⁴ For I write you out of much affliction and anguish of heart and with many tears, not to cause you pain but to let you know the abundant love that I have for you.

⁵ But if any one has caused pain, he has caused it not to me, but in some measure—not to put it too severely—to you all.

---

of one major portion of the letter: punishment to the offender who revolted against Paul (cf. 7:9-12); and (2) chapters 10—13 have no appropriate introduction which one would expect if this were an entire letter.

[4] Paul here indicates what his emotional state was when he wrote the severe letter. The **affliction, anguish of heart** and **tears** do not seem to be uncommon for Paul, as his ministry often involved this kind of response. Paul's speech to the Ephesian elders recalls his constant admonitions "with tears" (Acts 20:31). Paul recalls in 1 Thessalonians 3:7 that his ministry often involved "distress and affliction."

His purpose was not to multiply grief, but to cause his readers to **know the abundant love I have for you.** It was affection, not cold severity, that caused him to write. **Love** (*agapē*) was God's gift in Jesus Christ and is now the bond of the Christian community.

[5] Only now do we get partial information concerning the trouble at Corinth. Someone (*tis, ho toioutos*) has caused grief to Paul. It is extremely doubtful that this person is to be identified with the immoral man in 1 Corinthians 5:1; of such a person Paul could hardly have written that his only concern was in obedience to himself (vs. 9). Apparently the offender here has attacked Paul's work as apostle in a particularly offensive way. The revulsion could thus be felt as an insult to the entire community founded on Paul's preaching. Thus Paul says he **has caused pain . . . to you all.** The expression **not to put it too severely** (*hina mē epibarō*) uses the metaphor of a heavy burden (*barein*, "to carry a burden"). The idea is, "not to press this fact of my own injury too heavily—he has injured you all."

⁶ For such a one this punishment by the majority is enough;
⁷ so you should rather turn to forgive and comfort him, or
he may be overwhelmed by excessive sorrow. ⁸ So I beg
you to reaffirm your love for him.

---

[6] Titus has reported that the Corinthian church has
followed Paul's instructions fully in exercising discipline
on the offender (7:9ff.). The **majority** punished the offender. The word for **majority** (*pleiones*) does not necessarily mean that a minority of the church refused to repent. The word can also mean "the whole group." Paul's
satisfaction probably indicates that the entire church was
faithful in this matter.

The **punishment** (*epitimia*) was probably exclusion
from the community, as at 1 Corinthians 5:2. Paul is here
following the words of Jesus at Luke 17:3, "If your
brother sins against you, rebuke him; if he repents, forgive him." The punishment is **enough**; it has accom-
plished enough, since it has brought about the repentance of the offender.

[7] If the punishment has achieved its purpose, the
natural Christian response is to **forgive** (*charisasthai*) and
comfort (*parakalesai*). This forgiveness is based on the
forgiveness one has received in Christ (Col. 3:13); the
Christian response is to share this forgiveness. **Comfort**
has also the idea of "encouragement." Because Paul has
been comforted by God himself (1:4-7; 7:6, 7), he encourages the church to share this comfort. He has heard
from Titus that the offender, deeply grieved, was near
the point of despair. Paul wants the sorrow to be "the
godly sorrow that leads to repentance" (7:10).

[8] Paul does not here invoke his apostolic authority
and command the forgiveness; as an equal he begs them
to grant it. They are to **reaffirm** (*kuroō*) their love. The
word for **reaffirm** has the idea of validating. It is not
enough for the church to make a statement allowing the
man to reenter the church. By their actions they are to
validate their **love**.

⁹ For this is why I wrote, that I might test you and know whether you are obedient in everything. ¹⁰ Any one whom you forgive, I also forgive. What I have forgiven, if I have forgiven anything, has been for your sake in the presence of Christ,

---

[9] This passage is a little surprising. Paul has stated at 1:24 that he had no intention of intervening or "lording it over their faith." Now he says that their treatment of the offender was a test case of their obedience (see 10:6). The health of the church depended on their obedience in punishing the guilty one. The word **test** (*dokimē*) is used frequently in the New Testament. In Classical Greek it was used frequently of metals that had been tested in fire. Numerous tests are mentioned in the New Testament for the Christian. At 1 Corinthians 11:19, the **dokimoi** ("tested ones") are those who do not split into groups; at 2 Corinthians 9:13, they have been tested by their giving. Here the test is obedience. It is assumed here that any obedience to Paul is obedience to Christ.

[10] They had joined him in condemning; he now joins them in forgiving. The expression, **if I have forgiven anything**, is problematic. Certainly there is no question here of Paul's willingness to forgive. He may have in mind, "If I have anything to forgive." According to this view, Paul is here so gracious that he refuses to remember past injustices to him. A more probable view is that Paul is saying that the church has to take the initiative in forgiving and that he can only confirm it.

His forgiveness is **for your sake in the presence of Christ**. The expression **in the presence of Christ** is literally "in the face of Christ." *Prosōpon* literally means "face" (cf. 4:6), but can also mean "presence." Thus in 1 Corinthians 5:4, the church is to expel someone in view of Paul's "presence" (*prosōpon*). The face (*prosōpon*) of God is spoken of as approving or disapproving the actions of men (see 1 Peter 3:12). Here Paul forgives in view of the approving presence of Christ (see Col. 3:13).

¹¹ to keep Satan from gaining the advantage over us; for
we are not ignorant of his designs.
¹² When I came to Troas to preach the gospel of
Christ, a door was opened for me in the Lord; ¹³ but my
mind could not rest because I did not find my brother
Titus there. So I took leave of them and went on to Macedonia.

---

[11] The expulsion of the offender from the church
had the good intent of causing that person to repent and
be restored to the church. If, however, the church neg-
lected its responsibility to forgive, the advantage would
be taken by Satan. Paul's purpose is **to keep Satan from
gaining the advantage.** There was a purpose in such expulsion: to cause a person to "repent and come to know
the truth" (2 Tim. 2:25). If, however, the church is in-
sensitive to the repentance of the man, Satan would have
the **advantage** (see 2 Tim. 2:26). *Pleonektein* ("take advantage") has the idea of trickery or deceit. It would be
a loss to the church if the man's regret made him despair
and left him open to Satan's wiles.

The New Testament is full of warnings in the strug-
gle against Satan (cf. Rom. 16:20; 1 Cor. 7:5; 2 Cor.
11:14; 1 Thess. 2:18). **Satan** is the most common name,
although Paul occasionally uses the word *diabolos*
("devil"). **Satan** is the Hebrew word meaning "adver-
sary" or "prosecuting attorney." The warning here is
against Satan's deceitfulness (see also 11:14).

[12, 13] Paul nowhere tells a connected story of his
recent plans and travels. Attempts have been made to
discover this itinerary in the book of Acts, but such attempts are unsuccessful. He first planned to go from Ephesus through Macedonia to Corinth (1 Cor. 16:5). While
at Corinth on the painful visit, he decided to come back
there on his way to Macedonia (1:16). Further thought,
however, caused him to delay his plans in order to give
the Corinthian church time to repent (1:23). Thus he
returned to his original plan, sent the "stern" letter by
Titus to Corinth, and traveled north from Ephesus toward

Macedonia. Titus was to travel north from Corinth and east through Macedonia and meet Paul along a prearranged route.

Troas was one place where the meeting might have taken place. Probably there were mutual contacts there. Here Paul stayed at the time of his first journey into Greece (Acts 16:8), and he later halted there before going to Jerusalem (Acts 20:5, 6). Second Timothy 4:13 refers to items which Paul left at Troas.

At Troas, a **door was opened.** The idea of the door is a figurative expression in the New Testament for an opportunity, especially in missionary endeavors. A closed door means loss of opportunity (Rev. 3:7; Luke 13:25). The "open door" is more than once used as a figurative expression for opportunity (cf. Col. 4:3; 1 Cor. 16:9; Acts 14:27). It is God who opens the door by providing a favorable setting. Paul had an exceptional opportunity to preach at Troas; perhaps people were unusually receptive there.

The natural thing for Paul would have been to take advantage of the opportunity which was presented at Troas and to build a strong church there. But his **mind could not rest** (see 11:28). Literally, "I had no relaxation for my spirit" (*pneuma*). The same expression is used at 7:5, except there he says, "I had no relaxation for my body." The point is the same. Paul was too filled with anxiety over the Corinthian situation to become involved in another work at Troas.

He crossed to **Macedonia** to meet **Titus,** who had been sent with the stern letter. Titus is never mentioned in Acts, but from Paul's epistles we gather that he worked closely with Paul. He was a Greek by birth (Gal. 2:3), and he once accompanied Paul to Jerusalem (Gal. 2:1, 3). According to the epistle addressed to him, he played an important role in the organization of the churches of Crete.

At this point, as the reader is anticipating knowledge of the final outcome of Titus' visit, the narrative breaks off. The narrative of Paul's meeting with Titus is not

¹⁴ But thanks be to God, who in Christ always leads us in triumph, and through us spreads the fragrance of the knowledge of him everywhere.

---

resumed until 7:5. In fact, 7:5 fits perfectly to 2:13. It is very understandable that many scholars observe this interruption and conclude that 2:14—7:4 is a separate letter, inserted here by error. But this conclusion is hardly necessary. Paul frequently changes the subject abruptly and then returns to it. It is possible that a break in dictating occurred here and that Paul later wanted to enlarge on the subject of 2:14—7:4 before returning to this narrative.

[14] The **thanks be to God** is Paul's transition to the subject matter of verses 14-17. The expression indicates that good news from Titus came and that Paul was so overcome with the thanksgiving that he went on to enlarge the subject of his thanks. The remembrance of the victory of God's cause at Corinth causes Paul to expand his scope to the victory of God's cause everywhere.

God, in Christ, **leads us in triumph.** The verb *thriambeuō* ("lead in triumph") occurs only here and at Colossians 2:15. In the latter passage it is said that Christ in the cross and resurrection has "triumphed over" the principalities and powers. *Thriambeuō* suggests the image of victorious generals who led triumphal processionals after a great victory. Prisoners were led as captives and as public displays of the victory that was won. Thus Paul says that the success of the gospel is so great and so public that it compares with the triumphant processionals which were common. The purpose of these processionals was the public display which they offered. Paul's word here translated **spreads** is actually the word for "make manifest" (*phanerounti*). God's processional is on public display through the work of Paul. It is not certain whether Paul thinks of himself, according to the image, as the prisoner or the general. The image appears to fit better if Paul is here speaking of himself as a prisoner of God, as he elsewhere does (Phile. 1, 9). This idea that

¹⁵ **For we are the aroma of Christ to God among those who are being saved and among those who are perishing,**

God and Christ control his life and travel is another answer to those who have thought his change of plans arose from fickleness. Paul here thinks beyond his present plans to include the scope of his entire ministry. Thus the words **always** and **everywhere** show that he is thinking of his entire ministry.

What is manifest is the **fragrance of the knowledge of him.** The metaphor of **fragrance** may be suggested by his use of the image of the triumphal processional. Along the route of the conqueror, incense was released, creating a fragrance. The metaphor is also common in the language of sacrifice, by which it was thought that the fragrance from a sacrifice went to the gods and kindled a favorable attitude toward men. This language of sacrifice is also used at Ephesians 5:2 (cf. Phil. 4:18), where Christ is described as "a fragrant offering."

Paul's ministry is important here as he is the one who spreads the fragrance, confronting men with the knowledge of him and causing them to make a decision concerning Christ. Paul elsewhere in 2 Corinthians speaks of his ministry as the dissemination of **knowledge** (4:6; 10:5). Such **knowledge** is more than a recognition of the true God; it is acknowledgment of God through response to him.

[15] To those who disparage Paul's ministry, he responds here, **we are the aroma.** This is an interesting turn in the discussion, since at verse 14 the fragrance applies to the knowledge of God (or Christ). The RSV preserves the change which Paul has made in wording. In verse 14 he speaks of a fragrance (*osmē*), where here he speaks of an **aroma** (*euōdia*) *Osmē* applies to any smell, whether good or bad. *Euōdia* is generally used of sacrifices to denote a pleasant smell. The content which causes the aroma is Christ. Paul is the aroma wafted or filled by Christ.

Paul indicates that the one aroma produces quite different results. He is continuing here the figure of the

¹⁶ to one a fragrance from death to death, to the other a fragrance from life to life. Who is sufficient for these things? ¹⁷ For we are not, like so many, peddlers of God's word; but as men of sincerity, as commissioned by God, in the sight of God we speak in Christ.

---

victory processional. The incense at one time heralded the execution of the prisoners and the celebration of the victors. In the same way, the gospel has differing results on those who hear it. The gospel presents its hearers with a decision which determines whether they are being saved or are perishing. Similarly, the word of the cross presents different responses: to some it is folly, and to others it is the power of God (1 Cor. 1:18ff.).

[16] This smell is for some the stench of death. For others, it is a pleasant fragrance. The gospel produces opposite effects on those who hear it (cf. 1 Peter 2:7; Phil. 1:28; Rom. 9:18). The gospel confirms some in their sin; they reject it, and thus the end is death. It finds in others a response that leads to immense blessings.

The end of verse 16 carries the question, **Who is sufficient for these things?** or "Who is qualified for these things?" With issues so momentous, how can any man dare to carry on such a ministry? Paul would never boast of having any superior resources of his own. Indeed, it was God's mercy (2 Cor. 4:1), grace (1 Cor. 15:10), and trust (Gal. 2:7) that qualified Paul for his task. Just in case his readers think that Paul is arrogant or boastful, he adds at 3:5, "Our sufficiency is of God." Paul is **sufficient** through God's enabling power.

[17] Paul here answers the question of his sufficiency by contrasting himself to **peddlers** of God's word. **The many,** referred to here, are probably the false apostles who have been troubling the Corinthians (11:13). Paul is sufficient to the task, but they are not, as they are **not commissioned** by God.

Although we know little about the doctrines held by Paul's opponents, Paul tells us much about their manner. They practice cunning and deceit and tamper with God's word (4:2), and they prey on the people (11:13). Paul's accusation that they are **peddlers** is interesting. *Kapēleuontes* (**peddlers**) described those who made an illegitimate profit in retail trade. The word was used by philosophers to describe inauthentic philosophers who sold their teaching for money. The term is a natural one for Paul to use for his opponents, as he had heard it used to describe philosophers who were **peddlers**. Here it is possible that Paul is accusing them of teaching for money, a practice that was known in some circles. The fact that Paul has to defend himself in 2 Corinthians (11:7-9) for not taking money makes this conclusion likely. Certainly, he is also describing people who falsify the word by making additions to it, just as a commercial **peddler** (*kapēlos*) purchased pure wine and adulterated it with water. Thus **peddlers of God's word** here and those who were tampering with God's word at 4:2 were those who distorted the gospel. These were the people, according to 11:4, who preached "another Jesus."

By contrast, Paul acted **sincerely** (*eilikrineias*), with moral purity (see 1:12). The word expresses the opposite of the deceit Paul has attributed to his opponents. Instead of the word **commissioned**, the Greek has the simple expression **from God**. His ministry originated from God, not from his own cunning (see 4:1). His integrity is further assured by: (1) God's presence and (2) the fact that he speaks **in Christ**. His moral life is determined by his relationship to Jesus Christ and by the power of God's presence animating his life.

The Character of the Ministry, 3:1—7:16

The Ministry of the New Covenant, 3:1-18. The subject of Paul's ministry (2:14—7:4) forms a large parenthesis in Paul's discussion of his recent relations to the Corinthian church. This extended discussion has been necessitated by the crucial issue which Paul's opponents have raised. Paul's opponents have come to Corinth challenging his authority and claiming to be apostles. Since Paul is threatened by a challenge, it is important that he an-

¹ **Are we beginning to commend ourselves again? Or do we need, as some do, letters of recommendation to you, or from you?**

---

swer the fundamental question, "What is the nature of the Christian ministry?" The answer determines whether or not Paul is the legitimate apostle.

[1] Before going on in 3:4-6 to further discussion of his competence for the ministry, Paul answers the charge that he is an egotist who continues to **commend** himself; **again** indicates that previous charges of this nature had been leveled at Paul. Perhaps his stern letter evoked the charge that Paul constantly **commended** himself. The fact that *sunistanō* ("commend") occurs frequently in 2 Corinthians indicates that a great issue was at stake here. Paul accuses his opponents of commending themselves (10:12), while he denies that he commends himself (5:12). At the same time, he does admit that in certain ways he does commend himself; he does so by stating the truth (4:2) and by enduring affliction (6:4). In the final analysis, it is not the man who commends himself who is anything, but the man whom the Lord commends (10:18). It is this fact which makes Paul, and not his opponents, a legitimate apostle.

We notice here that Paul's opponents commended themselves by means of **letters of recommendation.** These are the "peddlers" mentioned in 2:17 and the "false apostles" of 11:12, 13. As outsiders, they needed such testimonials. Such letters of recommendation were especially common in the ancient world. Even Paul's letters often served that purpose (cf. Rom. 16:1, 2; 1 Cor. 16:10, 11). Apparently, the letters of recommendation were of special concern at Corinth. It is to be noted that it is in Romans and the Corinthian letters, all of which were connected with the Corinthian church (Romans was written from Corinth), that Paul uses his letter as a recommendation (see Acts 18:27). The custom of providing **letters of recommendation** was in wide use then, chiefly because false teachers often abused the confidence. But since, then

41

² You yourselves are our letter of recommendation, written on your ° hearts, to be known and read by all men; ³ and you show that you are a letter from Christ delivered by us, written not with ink but with the Spirit of the living God, not on tablets of stone but on tablets of human hearts.

° Other ancient authorities read *our*

---

as well as now, anyone could get a letter of recommendation, they did not mean much. Because Paul was the founder of the Corinthian church, his credentials were well established. He needed no such recommendations. It is not certain who commissioned these false apostles with letters of recommendation. Since they were Israelites (11:22), Jerusalem has often been conjectured as the place of origin for Paul's opponents (see Gal. 2:12).

[2] The Corinthian church is Paul's letter of recommendation. He needs no other credentials. The idea is similar to 1 Corinthians 9:2, where the church is described as the "seal" of his apostleship. The expression, **written on your hearts**, suggests the language of the Old Testament, especially Jeremiah 31:33. The prophet had expressed the hope for a future covenant written on human hearts, not on stone. Paul states that the Christian ministry participates in that new covenant, written on **hearts**. Heart here, as throughout the Bible, suggests the center of man's inner life, the functioning of his soul.

The phrase **known and read by all men** is here a play on words. The Greek *ginōskomenē kai anaginōskomenē* can best be translated "read and recognized." All the world can see Paul's work through the Corinthian church. This is the kind of claim Paul made for the Thessalonian and Roman churches (1 Thess. 1:8; Rom. 1:8). They had caused all men to see God's work.

[3] Paul's authenticity is seen in that the Corinthians **show** (*phaneroumenoi*) that they are the letter. The letter was written by Christ; Paul claims here to be only a servant. "Christ wrote the letter, and I acted as postman." The word for **delivered** is literally "served" or "adminis-

tered" (*diakonētheisa*). Paul's ministry (*diakonia*) has been challenged by his opponents who claim also to be "servants (*diakonoi*) of Christ" (11:23). For any who doubt the quality of Paul's ministry, he reminds them that, although Christ was the real founder of the church, he was the minister. They could not disparage Paul's ministry without disparaging Christ.

This passage is clothed in the language of the Old Testament. Anyone familiar with the Old Testament would readily know the images which Paul suggests. With one stroke, Paul contrasts the gospel (and thus the Christian ministry) with two items. This discussion began by contrasting the gospel to certain letters of recommendation. It is written **not with ink** (*melan,* "black ink," usually made with soot), as were the letters of recommendation, but with **the Spirit of God.** The expression **the Spirit of God** is the transition to Paul's second contrast. It was said (Ex. 31:18) that the Ten Commandments were written by the finger of God. Prophets like Ezekiel and Jeremiah, however, despaired at the inadequacy of this law to change man. Thus they looked forward to a new covenant authored by God's Spirit (Ezek. 36:26; 11:19). The involvement of the Spirit in Paul's ministry is seen further in verses 6-8, 17, 18.

The contrast goes further. This new covenant was not written on tablets of stone, like the old covenant (cf. Ex. 24:12; 31:18; 34:1). The covenant written on stone had been unable to renew and redeem life. It pointed to God's demand, but it gave no power to cause man to obey (see Ezek. 11:19). Thus Christ's epistle, the church, is written **on tablets of human hearts.** The expression is literally "fleshly hearts" (cf. Ezek. 36:26). Jeremiah saw the only hope for his people in the time when God would put his law "in their inward parts, and write it on their hearts" (Jer. 31:33). The Corinthians, Paul says, are living evidence that Jeremiah's prophecy has been fulfilled.

Paul begins at verse 3 a polemic against an improper interpretation of the Old Testament that continues through verse 18. The fact that at verse 1 Paul is obvi-

⁴ Such is the confidence that we have through Christ toward God. ⁵ Not that we are sufficient of ourselves to claim anything as coming from us; our sufficiency is from God, ⁶ who has qualified us to be ministers of a new covenant, not in a written code but in the Spirit; for the written code kills, but the Spirit gives life.

---

ously defending himself against the pseudo-apostles makes it likely that Paul throughout this section is defending himself against people who were using the Old Testament wrongly. Indeed, we know that his opponents are Jewish (11:22). It is probable here that when Paul uses the expressions **not with ink** and **not on tablets of stone,** he is contrasting himself to some who give a very positive interpretation of the law. Such an approach causes Paul to show the surpassing worth of his ministry, in comparison to the law.

[4, 5] Paul's confidence is no "self-commendation." His ministry comes **through Christ,** who has enabled him to feel confident **toward God,** i.e., in the presence of God. In verse 5, Paul answers the question posed at 2:16, where Paul asks, "Who is sufficient for these things?" His answer here is that it is God "who makes us sufficient" for this kind of ministry. Just as in considering the origin of salvation Paul freely confesses that "all this is from God" (5:18), and just as he says that "by the grace of God I am what I am" (1 Cor. 15:10), so here he says, "our sufficiency is of God." Paul's humble acknowledgment here that sufficiency comes from God is to be contrasted to opponents who "commend themselves" (3:1) and "compare themselves with one another" (10:12). They base their claim to be Christ's ministers on their sufficiency, which includes their gift of speech (11:6) and their spiritual gifts (12:1-8). Paul, by contrast, makes no claim for himself.

[6] The idea of sufficiency, twice expressed in verse 5, occurs again here, for the literal translation of the opening words here is, "who also made us sufficient." When

God called us into the Christian life and into service, he made us competent and qualified us to be **ministers**. The word **ministers** (*diakonous*) is translated in the New Testament as "deacon," as "servant," and as "minister." The word does not here refer to an official title, but to all who serve God. The subject of the nature of Paul's ministry is very much at issue in this context, as it is throughout 2 Corinthians. In fact, the word "minister" (and related forms of the word *diakonos*) occurs more in 2 Corinthians (twelve times) than in any other Pauline book. The reason is that Paul's opponents claim to be **ministers** (11:15, 23). Thus here, and in much of the book, Paul is eager to distinguish his ministry from the ministry of false teachers. His is the ministry of a **new covenant**. Thus Paul, by using the expression **new covenant**, appeals once more to Jeremiah 31:33, where the expression was first used. **New covenant** is a much more fortunate translation of *kainē diathēkē* than the KJV "New Testament." We generally think of a "testament" as something that becomes effective only after the death of one of the parties (this is the meaning of *diathēkē* at Hebrews 9:16, 17). A covenant is, however, an agreement between God and man. It is not an agreement between equals; it is an arrangement offered by God for the benefit of his people, who promise to fulfill certain requirements. That the era which began with Christ was the fulfillment of Jeremiah 31:33 is the conviction of the New Testament (cf. Heb. 9:15; Mark 14:24; Matt. 26:28; Gal. 4:24).

Jeremiah's prophecy spoke of the **new covenant** as a time when the hearts of men would be changed and would no longer be hearts of stone. These predictions, according to Paul, were fulfilled when the Holy Spirit was granted to believers. Thus the new covenant is one of the **Spirit**, and not a **written code** (*gramma*). Here, as elsewhere, the **written code** and the **Spirit** are in opposition (cf. Rom. 2:27ff.; Rom. 7 and 8).

Paul's word for **written code**, *gramma* (literally "letter"), can refer to the Pentateuch (see John 5:37), to

⁷ Now if the dispensation of death, carved in letters on stone, came with such splendor that the Israelites could not look at Moses' face because of its brightness, fading as this was,

---

formal education (John 7:15), or to correspondence by letter (Acts 28:21). Here the **written code** is equivalent to the law. According to Romans 7:9ff., the law brought knowledge of sin and death. It pointed to God's will but gave no power for man to achieve his will. The only release from this "law of sin and death" is the "law of the Spirit" (Rom. 8:2), which is set in contrast to the law which brings only condemnation (Rom. 8:1). Thus the written code kills because it had no power over the inward man for renewing his life.

The Spirit gives life, something which law is unable to do (Gal. 3:21). This **life** is a present possession of the Christian (see John 6:63), and is granted at baptism (Col. 2:13). **The Spirit gives life** by doing what the law could not do; it acts as a power in the inner man, empowering him to obey the will of God.

By connecting his ministry with the new covenant, Paul here contrasts the glory of his ministry with any "ministers" who give allegiance to the law. Those who still give allegiance to the letter, i.e., Paul's opponents, are loyal only to the dispensation which kills.

[7] The contrast which Paul gives in verse 6 is on a more fundamental level the contrast between the ministry of Paul and the ministry of Moses. The contrast in verse 6 leads to the more lengthy discussion at verses 7-18. Here Paul's ministry is compared to the ministry of Moses. Moses was the minister of the written code; Paul is the minister of the new covenant. Verses 7-18 have been described as "a Christian midrash [interpretation] of Exodus 34:29-35." Certainly the passage cannot be understood without reference to this narrative. Here Moses, the minister of the Old Covenant, radiates the glory of God because he has been with God. The brightness is so great that the children of Israel cannot bear to look at him.

⁸ **will not the dispensation of the Spirit be attended with greater splendor?**

Two dispensations are set in contrast. The word "ministry" (or the KJV "ministration") is to be preferred to **dispensation** as a translation of *diakonia*. The subject of discussion in this context is Paul's ministry (3:6; 4:1; 5:18), which he defends against his opponents. The ministry in which Moses was involved was indeed glorious, according to Paul, for Exodus 34:29-35 tells the story of Moses' glorious encounter with God. Yet it was still a ministry of **death** (*thanatos*) and **condemnation** (*katakrisis*, vs. 9). It pointed to man's sin but gave no power for redemption. By speaking of this ministry as **carved in letters of stone,** Paul sees the Ten Commandments as symbolic of the whole law.

A key word in verses 7-18 is the word "glory," translated **brightness** or **splendor.** Both words are here a translation of the Greek *doxa* which is used to mean "praise," "honor," or "fame." In the Bible the word is used to express the awesome majesty of God. This majesty, in the story of Moses that Paul is referring to here (Ex. 34:29-35) and elsewhere, is expressed as a brilliant, blinding light. Moses, as God's minister, participated in God's glory or **splendor,** reflecting his **brightness.** Thus the Israelites could not **look at Moses' face** (*atenisai,* the word for **look,** implies a steady gaze). In contrast to Israel, which could not look at Moses' face, Paul is involved in a ministry in which every Christian is able to look at the glory of Christ (3:18). His ministry is, therefore, superior to that of his opponents, who continue to emphasize the dispensation of death. The brightness was fading; the present participle *katargoumenēn* indicates that the process was going on at the very time Moses was talking to Israel. This **fading** is for Paul symbolic of the transient glory of that **dispensation,** or "ministry."

[8] The new ministry "gives life" instead of "death" (vs. 6). Moreover, it was eternal and not **fading.** It was written by the **Spirit** on human hearts, and not on stone.

47

⁹ For if there was splendor in the dispensation of condemnation, the dispensation of righteousness must far exceed it in splendor.

Thus it is only natural that its splendor should exceed the
splendor of the ministry that had already faded. It should
not escape notice here that, in comparing the ministry
(dispensation) of the new covenant with the ministry of
the old covenant, Paul assumes that he is no less a figure
than Moses (see 4:6). Moses personifies the Christian
ministry. Moses is, in a sense, a type of Paul. Yet the ministry of Paul is actually superior to the ministry of Moses.
This relationship of Moses and Paul is especially evident
at verse 14.

It may appear strange that Moses is here a type of
Paul rather than of Christ, since in 1 Corinthians 10:1ff.,
Moses is a type of Christ. The reason for the view expressed here is that Paul's opponents have a very positive
view of Moses' ministry. Paul's polemic against Moses'
ministry throughout this chapter suggests strongly that the
opponents thought of themselves as "servants of Moses" as
well as "servants of Christ" (11:23). Paul's argument also
suggests that the opponents have emphasized Moses' splendor and the continuing splendor of the law which Moses
represents. Consequently, Paul is eager to show the even
greater splendor of his ministry.

[9] Verse 9 is really a repetition, in parallel form, of
the thought of verses 7 and 8. In this verse the contrast
is between the condemnation (*katakrisis*) of the old covenant and the righteousness of the new covenant. The ministry of the old covenant leads to condemnation because,
by reason of sin, it brings only death. In Christ, however,
"there is no condemnation" (*katakrima*). In Christ, there
is righteousness (*dikaiosunē*). Righteousness, as characteristic of the Christian's relationship to Christ, is a favorite
word with Paul (cf. Rom. 1:17; 3:21; chap. 4). The word
never suggests something which man achieves by his own
efforts; it is a gift from God. One is made righteous on
the basis of Christ's work (Rom. 3:21-24). The word is a

¹⁰ Indeed, in this case, what once had splendor has come to have no splendor at all, because of the splendor that surpasses it. ¹¹ For if what faded away came with splendor, what is permanent must have more splendor.

¹² Since we have such a hope, we are very bold, ¹³ not like Moses, who put a veil over his face so that the Israelites might not see the end of the fading splendor.

---

judicial term, which implies that God acquits man when he is guilty. Only through Christ and his new covenant is this righteousness available.

[10] The glory of the old covenant (and of its ministers) was restricted. Literally, he says, "What has been glorified within limits" had no glory in comparison to the superabundant (*huperballousēs*) glory. Certainly, for Paul, the old covenant was from God and profitable for study (Rom. 15:4); but just as the light of the sun makes lesser lights seem as nothing, the new covenant is incomparable in its radiance.

[11] Verse 11 repeats the thought of verses 7-10. For the second time in this paragraph Paul uses the expression which literally is, "How much more?" (*pollō mallon,* cf. vs. 8, *pōs mallon*). The translation obscures this important phrase. The entire paragraph, however, centers around the idea: "if there was glory to Judaism, how much more glorious is the Christian ministry." This argument, from the lesser to the greater ("how much more") is a familiar rabbinical argument.

[12] Paul's hope rests on the facts of verses 7-11. The ministry to which he has been appointed is eternal and glorious. His boldness is a result of such a hope. His boldness, like his confidence (vs. 4), came from his faith that God has appointed him to a great ministry. This point is his defense against any who attack his ministry.

[13] Again we notice that Paul compares himself to Moses. Each symbolizes the covenant he administers. Moses' use of the veil was for Paul an indication of his lack of boldness. According to the narrative in Exodus (Ex. 34:33-35), Moses wore the veil when he was in the

¹⁴ **But their minds were hardened; for to this day, when they read the old covenant, that same veil remains unlifted, because only through Christ is it taken away.**

---

presence of the Israelites, but took it off when he was in the presence of God. The Exodus narrative makes no mention of Paul's statement here that the purpose of the veil was to prevent the Israelites from seeing the **end of the fading splendor.** But for Paul, the entire story symbolized the transient nature of Moses' ministry. There is a special reason for this emphasis on the transient nature of Moses' glory. Paul wants to emphasize to any who continue looking to Moses or to the law that whatever glory that dispensation ever had, it no longer exists. It is Paul's ministry, not that of his opponents, which is filled with glory.

[14] Verse 14 is a very abrupt transition to another thought. The Exodus narrative does not say that **their minds were hardened,** as Paul does here. This hardening of Israel's mind (or heart) is, however, a frequent theme in the Old Testament. The hardening which Paul sees among Jews has been with them from the beginning. This is the same kind of argument which Stephen used (Acts 7) in his defense. According to this view, the failure of the Jews to recognize Christ was due to their failure to perceive the intent of the law from the beginning.

When Paul said that **their minds were hardened,** he thought of his own day. One of the facts of greatest concern for Paul was the failure of the Jews to accept Christ (see Rom. 9—11). This failure he described as a hardening (Rom. 11:25), which would last until the conversion of the Gentiles. This hardening is evidenced in their inability to read the Old Covenant. The **veil** has blinded them. They do not see the intent of the Old Testament, since the Old Testament is fulfilled in Christ.

It is interesting how skillfully Paul varies the image of the veil. In the original story, the veil was on Moses. But since Moses symbolized that covenant, Paul implies in verse 14 that the veil is on the **old covenant.** In verse

¹⁵ Yes, to this day whenever Moses is read a veil lies over their minds; ¹⁶ but when a man turns to the Lord the veil is removed.

15, the veil is on their **hearts.** The image serves well to describe the obduracy of the Jewish people.

The phrase **old covenant** is used here of the entire Old Testament, and indeed is translated as "Old Testament" in the KJV. The expression was coined in the New Testament (cf. Heb. 9:15; Gal. 4:24).

Through Christ the veil is taken away. According to Exodus 34:34, quoted in verse 16, the veil was removed when Moses "turned to the Lord." The Old Testament word for **Lord** was in the Greek Bible *kurios.* This same word is used by Paul for Christ in the New Testament (see Phil. 2:11). Thus when Paul read in the Old Testament that Moses' veil was removed when he "turned to the Lord" (see vs. 16), he saw a connection to his present situation. When the Jews turned to the Lord, that is, to Jesus, they too would have the veil removed. When they are converted to Christ, they will see the true intent of the Old Testament.

Christ is here considered to be the key to understanding the Old Testament. This point was the united witness of the New Testament, and it was the focal point of discussion between Jews and Christians. The Jews searched the Scriptures, but they missed the point of the Scriptures, since the Scriptures testify to Jesus (John 5:39). Not only is Jesus here the fulfillment of Scripture, but only those who are converted to him can interpret Scripture. It is Christ, the risen Lord, who interprets the Old Testament within the community of Christians. The men on the road to Emmaus did not understand the Scriptures until the risen Lord interpreted them (Luke 24:27-32). Thus the veil is taken away when one accepts Christ, for only then does the risen Lord interpret the Scriptures.

[**15, 16**] Verses 15 and 16 repeat the thought of verse 14. One sees here (and in Rom. 9—11) what a severe problem the Jewish rejection of Christ was for Paul. Every

¹⁷ Now the Lord is the Spirit, and where the Spirit of the Lord is, there is freedom.

Sabbath **Moses is read** publicly in the synagogue. How could they fail to see that the Old Testament was fulfilled in Christ? Paul's answer is that they remain blinded by the **veil.** Here the **veil** is on their **minds** and not on the Scripture, as in verse 14. The word for mind here is actually *kardia,* which means "heart" (as in the KJV). But **minds** here is an adequate translation, since in the New Testament both "mind" and "heart" are used for the seat of intelligence, emotion, and will.

Verse 16 resembles, but does not quote literally, Exodus 34:34, which says that "when Moses went in before the Lord he took the veil off." For Paul, Moses is symbolic of all Israel, and thus when Israel **turns to the Lord,** i.e., is converted, the veil will be taken away for Israel. According to Romans 11:23-26, Paul held out the expectation that Israel would in fact turn to the Lord.

[17] Verses 17, 18 draw the conclusions as to what it means for the Christian who has the veil removed. Verse 17 in particular may seem to interrupt the thought of 7-18, since only this verse departs from the discussion of Moses and the veil, and since the discussion of the veil is resumed at verse 18. The function of verse 17 is important as a conclusion to the discussion. What is the result for the Christian who has had the veil removed? This verse provides the answer.

The expression **the Lord is the Spirit** certainly is unusual for Paul. Some have objected to Paul's identification of the Lord and the Holy Spirit, and have taken **Spirit** to refer not to the Holy Spirit but to Christ's essential nature as "spirit." Certainly Paul does not completely identify the Holy Spirit with Christ (2 Cor. 13:14). At the same time, Paul never gives any detailed treatment to the doctrine of the Trinity, and thus he makes no distinction between the functions of persons of the Trinity. What he says of Christ, he says also of the Holy Spirit. For instance, he speaks of Christ as the "first fruits" at

¹⁸ And we all, with unveiled face, beholding ^{*d*} the glory of the Lord, are being changed into his likeness from one degree of glory to another; for this comes from the Lord who is the Spirit.

^{*d*} Or *reflecting*

---

1 Corinthians 15:23. At Romans 8:23 the same word is used for the Holy Spirit. Christ dwells in the Christian (Gal. 2:20), as does the Spirit (Rom. 8:11). Paul's ministry is devoted to the Lord, i.e., Jesus. Such a ministry has an advantage which was not available to Moses; it is the ministry of the Spirit (cf. vss. 3, 6).

Identification of **Lord** and **Spirit** provides a transition from discussion of the **Lord** (verse 16) to the expression here, **where the Spirit of the Lord is, there is freedom.** Already Paul has said that the superiority of the new covenant comes from the fact that it is a covenant of the Spirit, and not of the letter (3:6). Here the characteristic of the **Spirit** is freedom.

On numerous occasions, Paul speaks of the **freedom** in Christ. It is a freedom from sin (Rom. 6:18-23) and a freedom from the oppressive law. It is a freedom from the scruples of other men (1 Cor. 9:19; 10:29). In this context Paul says that as long as one was under the old covenant he was blinded and enslaved. The law enslaved because it pointed to demands which no one could keep. **Freedom** came only with the new covenant, with the free gift of Jesus Christ and his Spirit as a power to live. To say that **where the Spirit of the Lord is there is freedom** is equivalent to Paul's saying at verse 6: "the Spirit gives life." A similar statement is made at Romans 8:2: "the law of the Spirit has made us free from the law of sin and death."

[18] Verse 18 continues the interpretation of Exodus 34:29-35. The entire comparison of the Christian ministry with the Mosaic ministry reaches its climax here. **We** refers to all Christians, and especially to apostolic leaders. The comparison to Moses is clear. Moses is a type of the apostolic ministry. Only Moses appeared before God **with**

53

unveiled face and partook of God's glory. In the Christian ministry, all "who turn to the Lord" (see vs. 16) are able to come with unveiled face. Consequently, Moses' ministry is inferior to the ministry in which Paul participates. If, then, Moses' ministry is inferior to Paul's, it follows that Paul's ministry is far superior to any who claim to be "servants of Moses."

Because of the superiority of the new covenant, Paul has already spoken of his boldness (vs. 12) and his confidence (vs. 4) before God. Now, with unveiled face, he beholds the glory of the Lord, as Moses did. Here the word translated beholding (*katoptrizomenoi*) can also be translated "reflecting." Since Moses both reflected and beheld God's glory, it is not certain which idea Paul is conveying. The context indicates that the Christian, beholding the mirror, sees something in the mirror which those who are not Christians cannot see: the glory of the Lord. Only those who have the Spirit have access to this wonderful sight.

The effect of looking intently at the glory of the Lord is that Christians are being changed (*metamorphoumetha*) into his likeness. *Metamorphoō*, from which we get the English "metamorphosis," is used here and in Romans 12:1 to speak of the transformation which takes place in the Christian life. It is a change to become in his likeness. Every Christian is a "reflection" of Christ. Paul's word for likeness or image is an important biblical word. Christ is the image (*eikōn*) of God (Col. 1:15; 2 Cor. 4:4). Just as Adam was made in the image of God (Gen. 1:27), Christ as the "second Adam" is God's image. The Christian is conformed to the image of Christ (Rom. 8:29). Consequently, just as Christ is the image of God, the Christian participates in this image also.

It is a change from one degree of glory to another. It is a constant process. The Christian, in the present age, participates in God's glory as did Moses. But the greater glory is still to come after God has completed his purpose. There is present glory, but there is a future consumma-

¹ **Therefore, having this ministry by the mercy of God,ᵉ we do not lose heart.**

ᵉ Greek *as we have received mercy*

---

tion. The transformation takes place now in the inward man, but is fully manifest only at the resurrection.

All of this amazing transformation was not available through man's unaided efforts; nor was it available through the old covenant. It is **from the Lord who is the Spirit.** By attributing the whole process of transformation to the Lord, Paul provides a fitting conclusion to this comparison to the two covenants or "administrations," thus enforcing his statement at verse 6 that "the Spirit gives life."

To any who question Paul's ministry, his rejoinder in verses 7-18 is that his ministry is greater than the greatest of all ministers of the old covenant, Moses. Indeed, Christianity, through the "life giving Spirit," is superior to the old covenant.

The Ministers as Earthen Vessels, 4:1-15. [1] Since 2:17, Paul has been discussing his fitness and integrity for the **ministry.** It is a ministry of the new covenant (3:6), and it is vastly superior to the ministry of the old legal order. He speaks of his task rather than his official position. **Therefore** connects the preceding discussion with what is to follow. Paul has discussed in chapter 3 the divine glory of his ministry. Here he goes on to discuss in practical terms what his ministry involves. **We** refers to Paul and his fellow workers. His ministry originated from the **mercy** of God. Paul uses the passive voice, which says literally, "We were given mercy." The same expression is used at 1 Timothy 1:16, where God showed **mercy** in converting Paul. God's **mercy** has also been shown in the act of salvation (Titus 3:5), and in the present comfort which he gives (Phil. 2:27). Paul here emphasizes the part that God's **mercy** played in his ministry as a defense against his opponents, who have said that Paul is incapable of a great ministry because of his weakness (10:10). Paul does not follow the manner of the opponents in making claims

² We have renounced disgraceful, underhanded ways; we refuse to practice cunning or to tamper with God's word, but by the open statement of the truth we would commend ourselves to every man's conscience in the sight of God.

for himself (see 10:12, 13). His only claim for himself is that his ministry comes from God (see 4:7). Thus he does not **lose heart.** Paul's expression for **lose heart** (*egkakein*) describes the experience of growing weary and of becoming discouraged. Jesus uses this expression when he says (Luke 18:1) that men should "pray always and not lose heart." Because Paul is involved in such a glorious ministry, no affliction can cause him severe discouragement (see vs. 16).

[2] Paul next proceeds to answer his opponents. **We have renounced disgraceful, underhanded ways.** Literally, he has renounced "secret things of shame," i.e., those secret intrigues which cause shame. His defense of his integrity, voiced at 1:15-22, is repeated here. As the next phrases show, Paul is not only defending himself, he is accusing his opponents of shameful, unethical behavior. He refuses **to practice cunning.** Paul's word for **cunning** (*panourgia*) can sometimes have a good connotation ("resourceful"), but here it has a bad connotation. According to 12:16, Paul's opponents accuse him of being **cunning.** At 11:3, this was the characteristic of the serpent. No one could use such **underhanded** ways in the service of a glorious covenant. He does not **tamper with God's word.** To **tamper** with God's word is equivalent to being a peddler of God's word at 2:17. The word translated **tamper** (*dolountes*) means literally to "beguile." To **tamper** is to be deceitful in one's ministry. Paul assures his readers that he has not used guile (see 1 Thess. 2:3). False teachers preached "another Jesus" (11:4), thus tampering with God's word. The expression **God's word** in the New Testament does not ordinarily refer to a collection of books (cf. 2:17; Acts 11:1; 1 Thess. 2:13; 1 Peter 1:23). **God's**

word (or "word of God") refers to the proclamation which centered in Christ, who is the Word (John 1:1).

He commends himself **by the open statement of the truth to every man's conscience.** The center of controversy between Paul and his opponents has been over whether Paul wrongfully commended himself (see notes on 3:1). His opponents may be deceitful, but he is not. His **open statement** (*phanerōsis*) of the truth is to be contrasted to his opponents who were "underhanded," or "secret" (*krupta*) in their dealings. Paul has been accused of preaching a veiled gospel (vs. 3). It is equally possible that Paul is attacking his opponents for being unintelligible. It is not obvious here whether Paul is defending himself or attacking his opponents. It is more likely that Paul is here making an attack. Verse 2 seems to be an attack on his deceitful opponents. He has already described them as "peddlers of God's word" (2:17).

Paul's ministry has been an open manifestation of God's truth. *Phanerōsis,* Paul's word for **open statement,** is used in 2 Corinthians (along with the verb *phaneroō*) to indicate the openness of his ministry. The word is used at 2:14 to say that God leads him in public triumph. The word is used again at 11:6, where Paul says that he has "made it plain" that he was not lacking in knowledge. When Paul contrasts his methods with the methods of his opponents, it is impossible to know whether there was some doctrinal issue at stake. What Paul wants to emphasize most is the difference between himself and his opponents, both of whom claim to be apostles and servants of Christ (11:13, 23). He "commends himself" to them (see 3:1), as they do, but not by their methods. He commends himself by his suffering (6:4ff.) and by his open statement of the truth.

His final appeal is to their **conscience,** as at 5:11. At 1:12, he appeals to his own conscience in defending his integrity; now he appeals to their conscience.

The **conscience** is the judging faculty of man which

³ And even if our gospel is veiled, it is veiled only to those who are perishing. ⁴ In their case the god of this world has blinded the minds of the unbelievers, to keep them from seeing the light of the gospel of the glory of Christ, who is the likeness of God.

---

can either condemn or acquit. Here he says (as at 5:11) that the conscience of those who know him will give an approving verdict as to his sincerity.

[3] Paul continues here his charge against his opponents. The expression, **even if our gospel is veiled,** could be read as a charge against Paul's preaching. But in view of Paul's attack on his opponents in verse 2, verse 3 is best understood as a continuation of the polemic. At 3:12-14, Paul said that those who read the Old Testament without reference to Christ were **veiled.** Here those who are **veiled** are Paul's opponents, who continue to over-emphasize Moses and the law. Paul declares that only the reprobate cannot grasp his message. They are the ones **who are perishing.** At 11:15 Paul says, "their end will correspond to their deeds." Those **who are perishing** are the opposite of those who are being saved (2:16), and the difference is made by their response to the gospel (1 Cor. 1:18). The word implies in the New Testament the eternal plunge into a hopeless death marked by tribulation and wrath (see Rom. 2:8).

[4] Paul sees this world as a battleground in which Satan and his hosts contend with God and his forces for the lives of men. To Paul, God is in final control, and Christ by his victory over sin and death has already broken the grip of Satan on mankind (Col. 2:15; Eph. 1:21). But the effect of this victory is not yet complete. Only believers know something of it. Paul is very aware in 2 Corinthians that destruction lies close at hand. His opponents are really Satan in disguise (11:13, 14). He counsels this congregation not to let Satan take the advantage (2:11). Here Satan is called **the god of this world.** Only here in the New Testament is Satan referred to as a god. This power of evil is called by different names in

the New Testament. Paul speaks of Belial (2 Cor. 6:15); of the rulers of this age (1 Cor. 2:8); and of the "prince of the power of the air" (Eph. 2:2). John's gospel speaks of the "ruler of this world" (John 12:31; 14:30; 16:11). According to the New Testament, the evil one is not equal to God. Other religions have conceived of the earth as the great battleground of the forces of good and evil (cf. Acts 26:18). In the New Testament, the only power which Satan has is the temporary power which God has granted until the final day. Then God will "put all enemies under his feet" (1 Cor. 15:24, 25).

Why do Paul's opponents not perceive his message and respond to it? **The god of this world has blinded their minds.** The idea of seeing (or not seeing) is often used in the New Testament to signify spiritual cognition (see Rom. 11:8). Not only are Jews blinded by the veil (3:15), unbelievers are also blinded. The word "unbeliever" (*apistos*) usually refers to pagans (cf. 1 Cor. 6:6; 7:12-15; 14:22-24). The word appears in 2 Corinthians only here and at 6:14, 15. At 6:14-15, the word seems to be used to describe Paul's opponents (see notes on 6:14). Since Paul is most concerned with his opponents (see vss. 2, 3), **the unbelievers** here are probably "the disloyal." To say that they are **blinded** is similar to saying that their message is veiled (vs. 3). They have remained blinded because of their failure to turn to the Lord, i.e., to see Christ from the right perspective (see 11:4).

Paul does not concern himself here with the question of the free will of these unbelievers who are **blinded.**

Light is a metaphor in the New Testament for God's revelation (cf. John 8:12). Thus the gospel provides the light of God's revelation to illuminate the darkness of human ignorance. Light and glory are roughly synonymous, since they are both visible expressions of God's nature. In Exodus 34:29-35, God's glory was manifested through a great light. **The glory of Christ** refers to the risen Christ, who is exalted to share God's glory. As the resurrected Lord, he "reflects God's glory" (Heb. 1:3). This idea of **the light of the gospel** is important in Paul's

⁵ For what we preach is not ourselves, but Jesus Christ as Lord, with ourselves as your servants ᶠ for Jesus' sake.
    ᶠ Or *slaves*

discussion with his opponents, since there is some indication that the opponents were describing themselves as servants of light (cf. 6:14; 11:14). Paul, however, saw himself as "a light to the Gentiles," in fulfillment of Isaiah 49:6 (Acts 12:47; cf. Acts 26:18).

Christ is here **the likeness of God.** Paul has already referred to Christians who become "transformed into his image" (3:18). In the book known as the Wisdom of Solomon, wisdom is described as God's image and reflection (Wisd. 7:26). In the New Testament, these words are applied to Jesus. He is the preexistent word (John 1:1) who existed in the "form of God" (Phil. 2:6). He is God's reflection (Heb. 1:3) and image (Col. 1:15). The image of God, which was once present in Adam (Gen. 1:27), is regained in Christ by the resurrection.

[5] Paul's opponents commended themselves (see 3:1). Paul himself finds it necessary to answer the charge that he commends himself (5:12). Thus here he says, **what we preach is not ourselves.** He has not been boastful; nor has he been excessively preoccupied with his own experiences as a Christian. He has had the ecstatic experience of being called up to the "third heaven" (12:2); but of this experience he does not boast. It may be that Paul's opponents were boasting of such experiences.

Preaching is the public proclamation of Christianity to the non-Christian world. The verb *kērussein* means "to proclaim." A *kērux* was a town crier, or herald, who delivered the news orally. Paul's message was plain: he preaches **Jesus Christ as Lord.** Only in scattered references from Paul's epistles are we told what was the content of Paul's preaching. In 1 Corinthians 1:23, Paul says that he preached "Christ and him crucified." In 1 Corinthians 15:3, Paul gives in outline form the substance of his preaching: "that Christ died for our sins in accordance with the Scriptures, that he was buried, and that he was raised on the third day in accordance with the Scriptures."

The church very early learned the succinct confession, "Jesus Christ is Lord" (Phil. 2:11; Rom. 10:9), in response to the preaching of Christ. The missionary sermons in the book of Acts show also that the content of first century preaching centered in the death and resurrection of Christ (cf. Acts 2:22-37; 13:26-47).

Paul preaches **Jesus Christ as Lord.** Paul's word for Lord (*kurios*) was an exceptionally rich word. In the Greek Old Testament, the word was used for God (see comments on 3:16). In the Greek world, the word was used of divine beings and of the emperor. It could also be used of a master who owned slaves. When Paul preached **Jesus Christ as Lord,** he was saying that Jesus was divine and that for the Christian he was the absolute master. Jesus became Lord and Christ at the resurrection (Acts 2:36; cf. Rom. 1:4). Because Jesus came in perfect obedience and died on the cross, God exalted him so that now every knee shall bow and every tongue confess that "Jesus Christ is Lord" (Phil. 2:11).

Christ is the equivalent in Greek for the Hebrew Messiah, and means "anointed one" (Acts 10:38). As such, the word was originally a title and not a proper name. In this passage, however, Paul uses **Christ** as a proper name.

Paul says, **with ourselves as your servants for Jesus' sake.** He does not "lord it over their faith" (1:24). He, as founder of that church, is merely a servant through whom Christ was proclaimed. **Servants** is an expression too weak to express the Greek *doulos.* Paul is a "bond slave." The natural relationship of servitude was one of lord and slave. Paul here does not claim to be the servant of Christ; he is their servant **for Jesus' sake.** The expression **for Jesus' sake** is literally "because of Jesus" or "on account of Jesus." Paul's relationship to Jesus Christ has brought him into relationship with them. A service to them is a service to Christ. It is to be noticed here that Paul shifts

⁶ For it is the God who said, "Let light shine out of
darkness," who has shone in our hearts to give the light
of the knowledge of the glory of God in the face of
Christ.

---

from "Jesus Christ" to Jesus. Paul does not usually refer
simply to Jesus; in this chapter, however, the name occurs again at 10, 11 and 14.

[6] Resuming the image of verse 4, Paul says some
eyes have not been blinded. Just as blindness is attributed
to powers outside man, perception of the truth comes only
by God's activity and not man's. No one can claim il-
lumination on his own. Perhaps Paul's opponents were
claiming to have some superior insight while claiming that
Paul was inferior in knowledge (see 11:6). Paul responds
by an appeal to Genesis 1:3. He gives the paraphrase:
it is the God who said, "Let light shine out of darkness."
Only God was the source of light in the beginning. And
just as he was the only source of light in the beginning,
he is the sole source of revelation now. The God of creation is the God of redemption. Thus he has shone in our
hearts. God has removed the blindness of those who have
turned to him. Paul's opponents are blinded; but Paul has
been granted light (see vs. 4). Our hearts seems to mean
that all Christians are included and not merely Paul.

Some have thought that Paul's language in verse 6
is an allusion to his experience of light on the Damascus
road. Since Paul is discussing the basis of his ministry, it
would not be unusual for him to refer to the Damascus
road experience (Acts 26:13ff.). But of primary importance is the experience of all Christians (see 3:18) who
have received God's light. God illuminates all who turn
to him. The light which illumines us is the knowledge of
the glory of God shining from the face of Jesus Christ. As
in verse 4, light and glory are almost synonymous. Paul
is eager to show that Christ is the only light. He is the
light (John 1:9) which "enlightens every man." His glory
is from God (John 1:14). Paul's emphasis on this light
from Christ is probably directed toward those who have

⁷ But we have this treasure in earthen vessels, to show that the transcendent power belongs to God and not to us.

---

emphasized Moses to the point of detracting from Christ. There is no light apart from Jesus Christ.

Paul claims here no private esoteric truths. He defends his ministry against his critics by claiming that he was commissioned by God. Indeed, the truth of his ministry is open to any who obey Christ, and thus he preaches no veiled gospel.

[7] Verses 7-18 are a continuation of Paul's defense of his ministry, which has as a theme the words of 3:5: "our sufficiency is of God." Paul describes in powerful terms the hope which caused him to persevere in seemingly impossible circumstances.

One theme seems to stand behind Paul's defense of his ministry: his own frailty and the power of God. His opponents may preach themselves (see 4:5) and commend themselves (3:1). They are boastful. Paul is aware that he is merely an earthen vessel. In the New Testament the idea of the vessel is a metaphor for a person. Paul is God's "chosen vessel" (Acts 9:15). The wife is the "weaker vessel" (1 Peter 3:7). Perhaps the figure was drawn from Genesis 2:7, where man is fashioned from the clay. In ancient times **earthen vessels** were symbols of weakness. These earthen vessels (*ostrakinoi*) were easily broken. In fact, much of the ancient writing was done on broken vessels (*ostraca*).

The gospel here is the **treasure.** The figure of a treasure is used in the New Testament for the immense worth of the gospel. The kingdom of God is so precious that, upon finding it, one responds like one who has found a treasure (Matt. 13:44). Jesus' disciples are to lay up treasures in heaven (Matt. 6:19-21). In Christ are hidden the treasures of wisdom and knowledge (Col. 2:3).

There is irony in this description of a **treasure in earthen vessels.** Who would store a treasure in something so fragile? There is a reason that God chose to communicate the gospel in this way: **to show that the transcendent**

⁸ **We are afflicted in every way, but not crushed; perplexed, but not driven to despair; ⁹ persecuted, but not
forsaken; struck down, but not destroyed;**

---

power belongs to God and not to us. Paul's frequent persecutions have shown his own frailty. His survival is attributed to one thing only: the power of God. The mark
of the true apostle is that he depends on God's **power**
(6:7). **Power** (*dunamis*) is very much a part of the
gospel message. The gospel is the "power unto salvation"
(Rom. 1:16). God manifested his power at the resurrection, and that same power is available to the Christian
(Eph. 1:19, 20). His aim for the Corinthians is that their
faith rest in God's power, not in human wisdom (1 Cor.
2:5).

Paul here and elsewhere sees that God's power is
available in human weakness. Christ "was crucified in
weakness, but lives by the power of God" (2 Cor. 13:4).
The death on the cross looked like weakness, but such
weakness gave opportunity for the working of God's
power. Paul sees his own weakness as opportunity for the
working of God's power (12:9). There is, therefore, a
purpose for storing the gospel in frail **earthen vessels.**
Only in weakness is God's **power** manifest.

[8, 9] By using graphic antitheses, Paul expresses in a
striking way his "optimistic pessimism." For each word
expressing his weakness, there is a corresponding word
for the power of God. Even in hopeless times of distress
God has preserved his life from the worst. What happened
in Asia is what continually happens (see 1:8). A literal
translation of 8a would be, "We are hemmed in, but not
crushed." Paul's word for **afflicted** (*thlipsis, thlibō*) means
literally "to press." In the New Testament the word is
used in the metaphorical sense of pressures brought about
by persecutions and mental anguish. Afflictions are a necessary part of the Christian life (see comments on 1:6).
But God never allows his servant to be **crushed** by the
pressures which the Christian ministry brings. Paul's word

¹⁰ always carrying in the body the death of Jesus, so that the life of Jesus may also be manifested in our bodies. ¹¹ For while we live we are always being given up to death for Jesus' sake, so that the life of Jesus may be manifested in our mortal flesh.

---

for crushed (*stenochōreo*) is used in 12:10 and translated "calamities"; he can endure such calamities, knowing that they are "in behalf of Christ" (12:10).

Verse 8b, perplexed, but not driven to despair, is in Greek a play on words (*aporoumenoi all' ouk exaporoumenoi*). Paul's word for despair (*exaporoumenoi*) is used only here and at 1:8, where he says that he "despaired of life itself." Literally, the word means "in a situation with no outlet." It describes here the situation of someone who was at his "wit's end." Though God allowed him to be in doubt, i.e., perplexed, there was always a way out.

At verse 9a, Paul is persecuted by men, but not forsaken by God. Religious persecution is to be expected; indeed, to be persecuted for Christ is a privilege (Matt. 5:10, 11; 1 Peter 1:6; 3:4). God, according to Hebrews 13:5, "never forsakes."

The last antithesis here is, struck down, but not destroyed. Phillips captures the idea with his translation, "knocked down but not knocked out." Struck down implies the blows dealt by the forces of evil in a battle. But the final death blow is not given; they are not destroyed. Although Paul's situation is often desperate, it is never hopeless. God's power is capable of overcoming any tribulation, even when human effort is incapable of seeing victory.

[10, 11] All of Paul's sufferings amount to participation in the death of Jesus. Paul thinks of the sufferings which preceded the death of Jesus. He knows that "a disciple is not above his master" (Matt. 10:24). Jesus had taught that the disciple must share the cross (Mark 8:34). Paul thus bears on his own body the marks of Jesus (Gal. 6:17). The Christian follows Jesus, who was "crucified in

¹² So death is at work in us, but life in you.

---

weakness, but lives by the power by God" (2 Cor. 13:4).
No one will experience the glorious resurrection without
first suffering with him (Rom. 8:17; cf. Phil. 3:10).

Always carrying . . . the death of Jesus indicates that
Paul as a frail earthen vessel on his missionary journeys is
following in his Lord's footsteps. Paul's opponents are
impressed by eloquence and worldly wisdom. The true
apostle is distinguished by his sufferings (see 6:4).

It is worthy of notice that Paul speaks here of **Jesus**
rather than the more familiar "Jesus Christ" (4:5) or
"Christ" (1 Cor. 15:3). **Jesus** refers to the Jesus of the
flesh, and not to the risen Lord. This change in terminology
is probably brought about by Paul's opponents. They
preach "another Jesus" (11:4), not "another Christ." This
emphasis on the name **Jesus** indicates that Paul's opponents
emphasize the **Jesus** of the flesh. They know him "from a
human point of view" (5:16). They preach **Jesus** without
his suffering and his cross. Their view of Jesus was evidently of one who was skilled in speech (11:6) and one
who was a wonderworker (12:12). They patterned themselves after this view, and not after the Jesus of the cross.

Paul, by contrast, sees suffering as the sign that he is
following Jesus. When he suffers, he is carrying in his body
the **death of Jesus.** He patterns himself after a suffering
Jesus.

The life of Jesus which is manifest in Paul is the life
of the risen Lord. By crucifying himself with Jesus, he can
say, "Christ lives within me" (Gal. 2:20). At Romans 8:10,
11, Paul says that it is the Spirit which raised up Christ
which also "gives life" to the Christian.

[12] In the resurrection of Jesus, Paul has seen a principle at work: human weakness, even death, can be transformed into life. In his work as apostle, Paul has been given
life by God in the midst of hopeless situations. The same
principle is true in Paul's relationship to the Corinthian
church. Paul's labors bring suffering to him but **life** to his
converts. The more he suffers, the more he is able to bring

[13] Since we have the same spirit of faith as he had who wrote, "I believed, and so I spoke," we too believe, and so we speak, [14] knowing that he who raised the Lord Jesus will raise us also with Jesus and bring us with you into his presence.

---

a quality of life to his converts (see 1:4-7). The **death** which works in Paul is the "fear of death." The **life** available to his readers is, as in verses 10, 11, the life which the risen Lord (Gal. 2:20) and the Spirit (Rom. 8:10, 11) give to the Christian.

[13] It takes great faith to undergo such sufferings and still to speak. Paul's faith has not wavered. The KJV has translated Paul's statement literally: "We have the same spirit of faith, according as it is written. . . ." Thus the literal translation does not tell us what the same spirit of faith applies to. It could apply to the spirit of faith of either the psalmist or the Corinthians. The RSV seems to provide the proper explanation: it is the same spirit of him who wrote, "I believed, and so I spoke." Paul quotes from the Septuagint Version of Psalm 116:10. The expression, preserved literally in the KJV, is "as it is written." This expression is used throughout the New Testament (and in the Dead Sea Scrolls and ancient legal documents) to cite an unimpeachable law or authority.

The psalm which Paul quotes is a description of how the psalmist maintained faith despite afflictions and adversity. Paul says here that he has kept faith by maintaining the same spirit of faith. Faith in the New Testament is much more than intellectual assent to the existence of God (or Christ); it is an attitude of trust. Even when there is adversity, the man of faith trusts in God's care for him.

[14] Paul can maintain faith through his afflictions because of a certainty: the knowledge that he who raised the Lord Jesus will raise us also with Jesus. In a number of instances in the New Testament, God is described as "he who raises Christ from the dead" (Rom. 4:24; 8:11; 1 Cor. 6:14; 1 Peter 1:21; see 2 Cor. 1:9 for the general description). According to the New Testament, the bless-

¹⁵ **For it is all for your sake, so that as grace extends to more and more people it may increase thanksgiving, to the glory of God.**

ings which are available are both present and future. Those who participate in Christ's death now in baptism also participate in his resurrection now. Paul says to the Colossians, "You were raised with him" (Col. 2:12; cf. Eph. 2:1-6). According to Romans 8:10, 11, the Spirit which raised up Christ is also working now in giving life to the believer. There is a sense, therefore, in which the resurrection has taken place. There were heretics in the first century who believed that "the resurrection is past already" (2 Tim. 2:18), i.e., that the present life in the Spirit was all the resurrection one could expect.

Paul affirms here that the resurrection is future. God **will raise us.** Christ is only the "first fruits" of the resurrection, i.e., the first installment (1 Cor. 15:23). The present possession of the Holy Spirit is only a guarantee (2 Cor. 1:22) of the future. The resurrection of Christ was the great moment when God guaranteed a future resurrection for the faithful (1 Cor. 15:23-28; 6:14; Rom. 6:5).

In Paul's labors he sees beyond the moment to the time when he will be reunited **with Jesus** and they (the church) will be united with Paul in his presence. Raised with Christ does not imply a temporal connotation. Christ has already been raised. With implies that Christ, Paul, and the church will all be together in one community. The idea of being with Christ is important for Paul. The Christian will, at the end, appear "with him in glory" (Col. 3:4). The final state will be that of being "with the Lord" (1 Thess. 4:17). The very opposite of this state will be "exclusion from the presence of the Lord" (2 Thess. 1:9).

[15] For the thought here, compare 1:3-7. It is interesting that Paul said in verses 11, 12 that his labor was "for Jesus' sake." Now it is **for your sake,** or "on your account." But one does not distinguish between work for men and work for God, since any labor for the church is a service

¹⁶ So we do not lose heart. Though our outer nature is wasting away, our inner nature is being renewed every day.

---

to Christ. The end result is that many people will be converted, i.e., grace may abound (cf. Rom. 5:20; 1 Tim. 1:14), so that it may increase thanksgiving to the glory of God. One cannot long continue suffering if that experience is senseless. But if suffering serves a definite goal, man's capacity to endure is almost limitless. Paul's suffering makes sense: he is serving God and man.

The Ministry and Judgment, 4:16-5:10. Verses 16-18 sound very much like the words of a Platonist. Philo would have agreed that "the things that are unseen are eternal." However, when we see this passage in its context, we are able to see that verses 16-18 are the hopeful statements of a missionary who has found here his reason for enduring.

[16] The expression, we do not lose heart, is a repetition from 4:1 where the same phrase is used. Here and at 4:1 Paul says literally, "we do not grow weary," because his suffering serves a great purpose. Throughout chapter 4, Paul has given reasons why discouragement did not stop him (see 4:1, 11). Here he gives a final reason.

The expression, our outer nature is wasting away, alludes to the experience of Paul the missionary. His ministry has caused him immense affliction (1:8; cf. 11:23ff.), which had also brought about a drain on his physical resources. Literally, Paul speaks of the "outward man" instead of the RSV outer nature, thus setting a contrast to the inward man. The "outward man" is the individual man in his creaturely mortality who is subject to decay and death.

There is another part of man. Here is the fact which encourages Paul: our inner nature is being renewed every day. The expression *esō* (inner nature, "inner man") is that part of man that is morally responsible, and therefore answerable to God (Rom. 7:22). This part of man's nature responds to God. God, in turn, gives strength through his Spirit in the "inner man" (Eph. 3:16). The "inner man"

¹⁷ for this slight momentary affliction is preparing for us an eternal weight of glory beyond all comparison, ¹⁸ because we look not to the things that are seen but to the things that are unseen; for the things that are seen are transient, but the things that are unseen are eternal.

---

is thus the place where man's spirit and God's Spirit meet. This inner nature is being renewed every day. The man who is being renewed is also a "new creature" (2 Cor. 5:17) who has also received the Holy Spirit as a guarantee. Paul is not here talking about a gradual development of one's spiritual life. He is simply thinking of his afflictions. He realizes that his work has depleted his bodily resources, but that each day he is renewed and strengthened as a Christian and lifted above all external pressures.

[17] Paul's mind bears heavily on his affliction (see 1:4-8). Yet, in contrast to the eternal weight of glory beyond all comparison, the affliction Paul knows is slight. In fact, the affliction has a positive result. It is preparing for us the eternal weight of glory. Paul's word for preparing (*katergazomai*) can mean "produce" or "equip." One does not merely endure the momentary affliction in order to receive a reward. The affliction prepares or "equips" one for the weight of glory. Christ did not experience the glory of the resurrection until he had suffered. In the same way, the suffering of the disciple leads to glory. The disciple can thus endure suffering with the knowledge that "the present suffering is not to be compared to the future glory" (Rom. 8:18). In addition, there is the awareness in the New Testament that suffering is useful for proving the genuineness of one's faith (1 Peter 1:7).

[18] Paul is not stating some general principle here. The things that are seen are the physical sufferings he endures. They are the outward nature and its decay. The things that are unseen include the renewal of the inner man (4:16) through the Holy Spirit and the hope for the eternal weight of glory. What Paul says here he says more succinctly at 5:7, "We walk by faith and not by sight." Because of this hope, Paul does not "lose heart" (4:1, 16).

¹ For we know that if the earthly tent we live in is
destroyed, we have a building from God, a house not made
with hands, eternal in the heavens.

---

[1] The chapter divisions separating chapters 4 and 5
are not entirely logical for the understanding of the text.
Indeed, 4:16-18 is a necessary presupposition for understanding 5:1-10. In 4:18, Paul turned his attention to that
which is eternal. In 5:1, his concern continues to be the
Christian's eternal possession. It is this thought of the
eternal possession which has prevented Paul from growing
discouraged during his afflictions.

Paul finds it necessary here to elaborate on the theme of
resurrection which he has already discussed at 1 Corinthians 15. One reason for this elaboration may have been
Paul's experience in Asia, in which he almost met death
(1:8). Such an experience could have brought about more
reflection on the subject of death and resurrection. But
the primary purpose of this discussion must be seen against
the entire context (2:14—7:4) of Paul's defense of his
ministry. Paul's opponents have attacked his ministry. At
4:16-18, Paul has shown how his ministry of suffering leads
to glory. Now he continues the theme of the hope that lies
beyond his sufferings.

The expression **for we know** connects the statement with
the discussion at 4:16-18. **We know** indicates that Paul is
not here giving any new information. He may be referring
to what he has already taught them; or he may simply be reflecting common knowledge. Jewish literature spoke of
"new dwelling places" reserved for the faithful in the future
age (see John 14:2). Paul contrasts here the **earthly tent**
with the **building** which comes **from God**. One is **earthly**
(*epigeios*); the other is **not made with hands** and, therefore, **eternal**. Paul's experience in Asia (see 1:8, 9) has
been a special reminder of the transient nature of earthly
existence and the great possibility that this earthly tent
may be **destroyed**.

The metaphor of the **tent** or the **building** is not unusual
in the Bible. Those "who dwell in houses of clay" are men-

71

tioned in Job 4:19. The language of this passage is very
similar to Jesus' statement at Mark 14:58: "Destroy this
temple that is made with hands, and in three days I will
build another, not made with hands." Jesus' statement, like
this passage, contrasts the physical body with the resurrection body. The metaphor of the **tent** for the body appears
also at 2 Peter 1:13. It appears to be very clear, therefore,
that Paul's use of words like **tent** or **building** was already
very common in passages which spoke of the last things.
The **tent** was useful in the ancient world for nomadic
people who kept no permanent home. Paul's use of the
term signifies the transitory nature of human life. Paul's
word for **destroy** (*kataluō*) also means "to take down." It
is the word for the dismantling of a tent when the time
comes to move on. He looks to the time when his tent, i.e.,
his body, will be replaced by a permanent structure, a
building. The more permanent building is the resurrection
body **not made with hands.**

The idea of the body as a **tent** was well known in
Greek thought. The Greek would have looked forward
with Paul to the dismantling of the bodily **tent.** The difference is that the Greek looked forward to the time when
he would be disembodied. For many, the body was thought
to be a tomb. In biblical thought, however, the body is
never considered evil. Paul looks forward to dismantling
this tent only so that he can assume the **building** from
God, the new body.

When Paul says that **we have** this building, he may
mean that the spiritual body is already prepared and wait-
ing for us. More likely, however, Paul is expressing the
complete assurance that we are to have it.

Apparently, Paul's use of the image of the **tent** follows
quite naturally the thoughts of chapters 3 and 4. In
chapter 3, Paul argued that the Christian dispensation was
a new Exodus. The discussion of the frailty and transitory
nature of life in chapter 4 could easily have led Paul to
think of the **tent** (Hebrew *sukkâh*) which was in Paul's
day a temporary dwelling place in which the Jew dwelt
for seven days at the Feast of the Tabernacles, a dwelling

² Here indeed we groan, and long to put on our heavenly dwelling, ³ so that by putting it on we may not be found naked.

---

designed to recall "the time which our forefathers spent in the wilderness and of the life they led in tents and booths." According to Paul, the Christian, like the forefathers, has to live in a **tent** before he reaches the promised land (cf. Lev. 23:42).

[2] In this present body we **groan.** Paul's word for **groan** also means to "sigh in an uncomfortable situation." The Christian groans in anticipation of "putting on" the heavenly dwelling. The present body is a body of death (Rom. 7:24), and it is "wasting away" (2 Cor. 4:16). Verse 4 continues the idea of the present groaning. The thought resembles very closely the idea expressed in Romans 8:23, where Paul says, "we . . . groan inwardly as we wait for the adoption as sons, the redemption of our bodies." Paul's assurance is here that the Christian has already received the "firstfruits" (Rom. 8:23) or "guarantee" (2 Cor. 5:5). But the fact that there is more to come gives him hope.

He wants to **put on** the heavenly dwelling. Paul is here mixing two metaphors in order to make his point. The metaphor of "putting on" is drawn from the act of putting on clothes. The Christian has already **put on** Christ (Gal. 3:27) and the "new man" (Col. 3:10) in baptism. He has yet to **put on** the glorious body. The second metaphor is that of the **dwelling** which, as was noted in comments on 5:1, was a common image for the future life.

[3] Paul explains in verse 3 that by **putting on** the dwelling they may **not be found naked.** Paul had first used the idea of nakedness (*gumnotēs*) with reference to death in 1 Corinthians 15:37. "And what you saw is not the body which is to be, but a bare (naked) kernel. . . . But God gives it a body as he has chosen. . . ." Some have thought Paul's reference to nakedness an assertion of the doctrine of an intermediate state of the dead in which the believer was in a disembodied state of nakedness. This view is hardly satisfactory, however. Jewish literature spoke

⁴ **For while we are still in this tent, we sigh with anxiety; not that we would be unclothed, but that we would be further clothed, so that what is mortal may be swallowed up by life.**

of nakedness as the state of the unbeliever. Besides, according to Philippians 1:23, Paul anticipated no intervening state of the dead.

Very likely Paul is clarifying the thought of 1 Corinthians 15:37. There is some anxiety in the minds of his readers over what happens at death. In 1 Corinthians 15:37 Paul may have left the impression that there is a period of nakedness. Here Paul assures the Corinthians that God will clothe them with the resurrection body. Paul does not distinguish here between the moment of death and the second coming of Christ. He is not concerned about whether or not there is an intermediate state of the dead. Rather, he is concerned with the ultimate condition of God's people. His purpose is to offer hope to the Corinthians who have been asking questions about death.

[4] Paul repeats here the thought of the present "groaning" (vs. 2) in this body. It is with anxiety. The KJV has retained the more literal translation of anxiety with the expression, "being burdened." The word is used of excessive physical burdens (see Matt. 26:43). But it can also refer to mental burdens, and thus anxiety is a proper translation. Paul uses the same word at 1:8, when he says, "We were . . . crushed." The anxiety is fully explained by such passages as 1:8 and 4:7-12. It is to be noticed here that, although Paul is presently burdened with anxiety, what he looks forward to is not escape. He does not simply want to be stripped (or unclothed) of the misery that bodily life involves. He wants to be further clothed, i.e., to receive the resurrection body. The word for further clothed (*ependusasthai*) means "to put on over" something else. Evidently, Paul speaks of the resurrection body that is "put on over" the existing physical frame. Paul's attitude toward death is hopeful; he thinks of death as entrance into the presence of Christ (see 4:14).

74

⁵ He who has prepared us for this very thing is God, who has given us the Spirit as a guarantee.

⁶ So we are always of good courage; we know that while we are at home in the body we are away from the Lord, ⁷ for we walk by faith, not by sight. ⁸ We are of good courage, and we would rather be away from the body and at home with the Lord.

Paul's description of human life as **mortal** was a common designation of men among Greeks. Men were mortal in contrast to gods who were immortal.

[5] **This very thing** refers back to verse 4, the final replacement of the frail body by the resurrection body. Paul never ceases to give the credit to God. Thus he says **God has prepared us.** Paul's word for **prepare** (*katergazomai*) usually has as subject God or Christ (cf. Rom. 15:18; 2 Cor. 12:12). Though human instruments are employed (see 12:12), it is "God who works" (Phil. 2:12). Paul here uses the aorist participle, which indicates a once-for-all action, not a continual process. Thus God **prepared** us at baptism through the gift of the **Spirit.** As at 1:22 (cf. Eph. 1:14), Paul speaks of the Spirit as a **guarantee** of the future inheritance. The Christian has already "the first fruits" of the Spirit (Rom. 8:23), but groans for the consummation (see comments on 1:22). The Spirit serves as **guarantee** because it is through the Spirit that we will be raised (Rom. 8:11).

[6, 8] Verses 6-10 state in different terms this longing for the new existence which has been mentioned in verses 1-5. His language here is not in terms of a building or dwelling; he speaks in terms of absence from the Lord. **So** refers to verse 5 and the hope enunciated there. Regardless of the affliction, he is **always** (*pantote*) **of good courage.** Verses 6 and 8 describe this **good courage** (*tharrountes,* "being of good courage"). This courage is supplied by the Spirit (vs. 5) and by **faith** (vs. 7).

Two modes of existence are mentioned here and at verse 8. To be **at home in the body** is to be **away from the Lord.** To be **at home with the Lord** is to be away from

⁹ So whether we are at home or away, we make it our aim to please him. ¹⁰ For we must all appear before the judgment seat of Christ, so that each one may receive good or evil, according to what he has done in the body.

---

the body. To live **in the body** is the same as to inhabit the earthly tent (5:1). Full fellowship with the Lord is possible only without bodily existence. This full fellowship would be **to walk by sight** (vs. 7). There is, however, partial fellowship right now in this body. It is created by **faith.**

[7] Verse 7 is a parenthesis in Paul's discussion, by which he explains what it means to be away from the Lord. The period of the resurrection body will be the time of **sight** when **faith** will not be necessary. The thought is similar to 1 Corinthians 13:12, "Now we see in a mirror, darkly, but then face to face." Also similar is Romans 8:24, "Hope that is seen is not hope. For who hopes for what he sees?" It is said of Moses (Num. 12:8) that he spoke "mouth to mouth" and "by sight" with the Lord. Paul anticipates the day when **faith** and hope will give way to full fellowship with Christ, when we will **walk by sight.**

[9] Verse 9 is Paul's solution to the practical problem of verses 6 and 8. Whether **at home or away,** Paul's ambition is to be pleasing to God. An excellent commentary on this passage is Philippians 1:18-26, where Paul says that although he prefers to be with Christ, his existence in the flesh is more necessary for others.

The goal of the Christian's life is **to please him.** He should present his body as a living sacrifice . . . pleasing to God (Rom. 12:1). The Christian should test what is pleasing to him (Eph. 5:10).

[10] **The judgment seat of Christ** is the same as God's judgment. According to the New Testament, all judgment has been committed to the Son (John 5:22, 27; Acts 10:42; 17:31; 24:25). The **for** shows Paul's reason for wanting to please him (vs. 9). The **we . . . all** refers to all Christians. **We must all appear,** "be made manifest," have our life laid open for scrutiny (*phanerōthēnai* is translated "dis-

¹¹ **Therefore, knowing the fear of the Lord, we persuade men; but what we are is known to God, and I hope it is known also to your conscience.**

---

close" by RSV at 1 Cor. 4:5). All men will, according to Paul, be judged (Rom. 2:6-8). Here, as at Romans 14:10, he speaks of the judgment of Christians.

Judgment will be based on what deeds one has done in the body. We know enough of Paul's doctrine of grace (see Eph. 2:8) to know that Paul had no idea of works salvation. Salvation was a gift, and therefore it could not be earned. At the same time, Paul taught that every man was under obligation to respond to this grace through good deeds. At 11:15, he says of his opponents, "Their end will correspond to their deeds." The obedient disciple will have something to be proud of in the day of Christ (Phil. 2:16).

[11] The following section (5:11—6:13) gives a further indication of Paul's conception of his ministry and his relationship to churches which he founded. Again he finds it necessary to defend his conduct and his apostleship. His integrity has been questioned by his opponents; but Paul knows that before God his ministry has been conducted with integrity.

Verse 11 provides the transition from the discussion of the resurrection to the subject of Paul's ministry. **Therefore** here refers to the discussion of verses 1-10; because of the certainty of judgment, Paul persuades men. **The fear of the Lord** is certainly not **terror**, as the KJV translates. It is to be understood in the same way as **fear of the Lord** is used throughout the Bible; it is reverential awe and respect. He persuades men of the urgency and truth of the message which has been entrusted to him. However, he has been accused of appealing to men in the wrong way (vs. 12). Probably, as at Galatians 1:10, he has been accused of trying to please (*peithō*, the same word that is translated **persuade** here) men and not God. Men may question this conduct, but **what we are is known to God.** Verse 10 states that at the last we shall all be

77

¹² We are not commending ourselves to you again but giving you cause to be proud of us, so that you may be able to answer those who pride themselves on a man's position and not on his heart. ¹³ For if we are beside ourselves, it is for God; if we are in our right mind, it is for you.

---

made manifest (*phanerōthēnai*) before God. Paul always works "in the sight of God" (2:17). Here Paul says that he is already **known** or "manifest" (*pephanerōmetha*) to God. In the same way, he hopes to be **known** or "manifest" (*pephanerōmetha*) to their **conscience**. According to 4:2, he has appealed to every man's conscience in the sight of God. He has confidence that if men follow their consciences, he will be **known** to them and accepted by them, just as he has been **known** and accepted by God.

[12] Throughout this letter Paul is sensitive to the charge that he commends himself (cf. 3:1; 4:2; 6:4). The word **again**, here and at 3:1, indicates that in an earlier letter he had boasted about his work in such a way as to arouse criticism from his opponents (see 11:16—12:13). Here Paul wishes to give the Corinthians an opportunity or **cause** to take up his defense in order for the church to be able to answer those who boast in outward **position**. Undoubtedly, they boasted of their personal knowledge of Jesus, their Jewish descent, and of their many labors (cf. 10:1ff.; 11:23ff.).

[13] Verse 13 reveals a particular controversy which Paul had with his opponents. Paul contrasts being in his **right mind** with being **beside ourselves**. The word translated **beside ourselves** is *existēmi*. It was the word which Jesus' opponents used against him (Mark 3:21). The charge meant that they considered Jesus mentally deranged. Thus it is possible that Paul is here answering the charge that he is eccentric in his assertion of authority.

The word also signifies "ecstasy," as in the use of spiritual gifts. It is to be remembered that Paul has to confront the issue of ecstatic, spiritual experiences in both epistles to Corinth (1 Cor. 12, 14; 2 Cor. 12:1-8). The most

¹⁴ For the love of Christ controls us, because we are convinced that one has died for all; therefore all have died.

---

likely view is that Paul's opponents have boasted of their ecstatic experiences and have used these experiences only to commend themselves. They have criticized Paul's use of the spiritual gifts, causing Paul to defend himself at 12:1-8. His response here is the same as in 1 Corinthians 14:2, 18. Spiritual gifts are useful only if devoted to God. Paul's opponents use "ecstasy" to commend themselves; Paul is "ecstatic," i.e., beside himself **for God.** He is in his **right mind** for the church (see 1 Cor. 14:19).

[14] Paul here explains why his ministry is for you, i.e., the Corinthians. Christianity is a corporate experience, as "no one lives to himself" (Rom. 14:7, 8). Paul's opponents at Corinth, especially those who prized ecstatic gifts, were concerned only with the individual's relation to God; they were unconcerned about the corporate experience of the church (see 1 Cor. 14:2-5). The reason Christianity is corporate and not individual is to be found in the very source of the Christian faith: the death of Christ. Christ's death was **for all.** He was the representative of every man in his death, just as Adam was the representative of every man in his sin (cf. Rom. 5:12-19; 1 Cor. 15:45-50). Here was the central aspect of Paul's teaching about the death of Christ. Paul said that his death was "for our sins" (1 Cor. 15:3) and "for me" (Gal. 2:20). Paul's statement, **therefore all died,** reinforces the fact that Christ was the representative of every Christian. Through discipleship (Gal. 2:20) and baptism (Rom. 6:4ff.), the Christian participates in Christ's death.

Paul's ministry finds its meaning in the death of Christ. The reason that the opponents of Paul "commend themselves" (5:12) is that they do not properly understand the nature of the death of Christ. Since Paul does understand the death of Christ, he lives for others.

Paul speaks of the love of God and the **love of Christ** interchangeably. This is the love which comes from Christ

¹⁵ And he died for all, that those who live might live no longer for themselves but for him who for their sake died and was raised.

¹⁶ From now on, therefore, we regard no one from a human point of view; even though we once regarded Christ from a human point of view, we regard him thus no longer.

---

that is spoken of. This love was manifested most clearly in the cross (Rom. 5:8). The fact of this love was so overwhelming that it is for Paul a motivating power to live a good life (cf. Rom. 8:28-31; 5:5).

[15] Paul has in mind both the charge of his opponents that he commends himself (5:12) and their behavior in living for themselves. If one takes the cross of Christ seriously, he will see that Jesus **died for all.** If Christians imitate Christ, that will be the end of living **for themselves.** It is thus in living **for themselves** that Paul's opponents invalidate their claim to be apostles. It is in living for others that Paul shows that he is a true follower of Christ. When the Christian dies (vs. 14), he dies to the old selfish nature; he is raised then to live in imitation of Christ. The way one can live **for him who died and was raised** is to live to build up the church, which is his body (see Rom. 14:7-8).

[16] The transition from 15 to 16 is rather abrupt. What does this **human point of view** have to do with Christ's death? The **human point of view** is literally a view that is "fleshly" or "worldly" (*kata sarka*). Paul's opponents have seen Paul's weakness and humility (10:1, 2) and have concluded that he is "fleshly" (10:2). Here Paul admits that before he became a Christian or a "new creature" (5:17) he did have this human point of view, i.e., he looked at Jesus from a worldly perspective. That worldly perspective or **human point of view** is the opposite of the point of view Paul gives in 5:16-21. It has no concern for the cross of Christ; one remembers that at 1 Corinthians 1:18-23, Paul says that the cross is foolishness to the worldly mind. This **human point of** view can see no value

¹⁷ Therefore, if any one is in Christ, he is a new creation;^g
the old has passed away, behold, the new has come. ¹⁸ All
this is from God, who through Christ reconciled us to himself and gave us the ministry of reconciliation; ¹⁹ that is,
^g Or *creature*

---

in the cross; certainly the opponents do not preach that
God reconciles through the cross (5:18, 19), or that he
forgives through the cross (5:21).

The opponents, however, preach Jesus. Yet he is "another Jesus" to them (11:4). He is not the Jesus of the
cross. The human point of view is to see Jesus as a
wonder-worker, a prophet, or a teacher. Since the opponents of Paul see a Jesus without the cross, it is natural
that they consider the suffering that Paul has experienced
useless. They have modeled themselves after their view of
Jesus: a Jesus without suffering.

[17] In verses 17-21, Paul elaborates on the blessings
available for those who live according to the Spirit. Those
who have obeyed Christ are **in Christ**. In a few instances
Paul says that Christ is "in you" (cf. Col. 1:27; Rom. 8:10;
2 Cor. 13:5). More commonly, the Christian is described as
in Christ. The Christian, being **in Christ**, is, as a result of
his baptism, a part of the body of Christ.

Such a person in Christ **is a new creation**. Jewish be-
lief was that in the last days God would restore the perfection of the original creation. God would bring in new
heavens and new earth by an act of a new creation (Isa.
65:17f.; 66:22; 2 Peter 3:13). Thus in the New Testament
one who obeys Christ is a "new man" (Eph. 4:24; cf. Col.
3:10). Neither circumcision nor uncircumcision matters, but
what counts is a "new creation" (Gal. 6:15). The **new
creation** is contrary to the human point of view (vs. 16).
It is a life of the Spirit (see Rom. 8:10-11).

The connection between 17a and 17b is not obvious.
The point is apparently that for the believer in his experience the **old has passed away**.

[18] **All this** new creation and redemption is **from God.**

81

God was in Christ reconciling ᵃ the world to himself, not counting their trespasses against them, and entrusting to us the message of reconciliation.
ᵃ Or *in Christ God was reconciling*

Paul is extremely careful in 2 Corinthians to give all of the credit to God. Christ does not act apart from God, nor does man merit his redemption. The Greek myth has the savior Prometheus acting in behalf of man but in opposition to God. For Paul, the cross signified not only the love of Christ, but also the love of God.

The result of Christ's activity at the cross is **reconciliation.** The metaphor is that of making peace after war or being readmitted to the presence and favor of our rightful sovereign after we have rebelled against him. It was through sin that man became alienated from God and from man (Isa. 59:1ff.). "We were," according to Romans 5:10, "enemies of God" (see Col. 1:21). Through Christ, Jew and Gentile can be **reconciled** in one body (Eph. 2:12-17). Man was in no position to bring about the reconciliation, so God **reconciled us to himself.** Only through Christ, therefore, is there "peace with God" (Rom. 5:1).

The church, and specifically Paul, has a **ministry of reconciliation** and a "message of reconciliation" (vs. 19), so that it implores men, "Be reconciled to God" (vs. 20). It was said of Jesus that he "preached peace to all men" (Eph. 2:17). This reconciling activity is continued in the church by words and deeds.

[19] The words **that is** introduce a restatement of the heart of Paul's message from verse 18. It was sin which caused the alienation between God and man. Therefore, Paul says that God was **not counting their trespasses against them.** Paul's word for **counting,** *logizomai,* is an accountant's word. It implies marking down misdeeds as a debit charge. God did not count **trespasses;** he freely forgave.

It was the **world** (*kosmos*) that God reconciled. According to Paul, the created universe was reconciled to Christ (Col. 1:20); here, however, he has in mind the **world** of men (see John 3:16).

²⁰ So we are ambassadors for Christ, God making his appeal through us. We beseech you on behalf of Christ, be reconciled to God. ²¹ For our sake he made him to be sin who knew no sin, so that in him we might become the righteousness of God.

¹ Working together with him, then, we entreat you not to accept the grace of God in vain.

---

[20] Paul's view of his ministry is more fully explained here. **We are ambassadors of Christ.** In this grand scheme God has a place for his earthen vessels. They are envoys or **ambassadors** (see Eph. 6:20). An ambassador is commissioned by a sovereign to speak on his behalf. This word indicates responsibility and authority. His appeal to **be reconciled** calls men to get rid of the sin which causes separation from God.

[21] This verse tells how reconciliation has been made possible. The irony is that the one **who knew no sin** became identified with sin so that those who are sinners might be identified with righteousness. The word "know" in Hebrew often meant "experience." Thus Paul says, "He who experienced no sin." The sinlessness of Jesus is affirmed throughout the New Testament (cf. Heb. 4:15; 1 Peter 2:22; John 8:46; Matt. 4:1-13). God has placed on the sinless Jesus the sins of humanity (John 1:29; Rom. 3:25; 1 Cor. 15:3). Man was under the curse (Gal. 3:13), but Christ took the curse upon himself.

Christ became **sin** by participating in the human condition. In this way "God condemned sin in the flesh" (Rom. 8:3). At the cross he participated in our sin, but made us righteous. **Righteousness** cannot be gained through works or through adherence to law (Rom. 3:21-25). **The righteousness of God** is revealed in Christ; it is available to his people through faith (Rom. 3:22), not through human effort.

[1] As God's servant, Paul never worked alone. His ministry was a "collaboration" or **working together.** The Greek does not say with whom Paul is working. Conceivably, he could intend to supply "with you," as if his

² For he says,
  "At the acceptable time I have listened to you,
  and helped you on the day of salvation."
Behold, now is the acceptable time; behold, now is the
day of salvation.

---

ministry were a sharing with the Corinthians. The RSV
and KJV supply the words **with him,** i.e., God. Undoubtedly, this is the most plausible idea. At 5:20, Paul has
said that he was God's ambassador and that God was
making his appeal through him. Because Paul is **working
together** with God, he can make the exhortations which
follow. One may compare also Philippians 2:13, where
Paul says, "It is God who works in you."

At 5:20, Paul has said, "God making his appeal. . . ."
Here he says, **We entreat you.** The same Greek word
stands behind "entreat" and "make appeal" (vs. 20). It
is the word *parakalein.* The word is often used for exhortation in the public proclamation; it often carries the idea of
"wooing." Whereas preaching (see comments on 4:5)
carries more the idea of an announcement of the good news,
to entreat is to make an appeal for response. Paul's point
here, as at 5:20, is to add authority to his appeal by showing that this is also God's appeal.

The appeal is **not to accept the grace of God in vain.**
Although grace is free and salvation cannot be earned,
there is always the response to God's grace which is important. It is possible that one who is saved by **grace** will
see the abundance of God's **grace** and therefore conclude
that **grace** is cheap. All of God's reconciling activity at the
cross would be **in vain** (*kenos*) if his grace were not received with thanksgiving. There is a danger that the Corinthians may lose that original enthusiasm which they once
had for Christianity (cf. 13:5; Gal. 3:4). If they do not
meet their responsibilities, Christ will have died **in vain.**

[2] We expect a detailed elaboration from Paul of the
content of verse 1. However, the word *dechesthai,* "to receive," reminds Paul of an important Old Testament text

which serves to emphasize the gravity of the situation. The expression, **he says,** means here, "God says." The passage is taken from Isaiah 49:8, and is quoted from the Septuagint, the Greek version of the Old Testament. In the Old Testament, the meaning was that God had heard the cries of the servant that his work had been in vain (Isa. 49:4). God, through his servant, was bringing in divine aid. Thus Paul applies this passage to their present circumstances, insisting that **the day of salvation** was present. Because the salvation was being offered, they were no longer to labor in vain (vs. 1; cf. Isa. 49:4). It was an urgent matter to accept God's salvation when it arrived.

Paul understands himself as nothing less than the agent of this **day of salvation.** He is God's ambassador (5:20), and God's appeal is made through Paul. The New Testament affirms elsewhere (cf. Acts 13:47; Gal. 1:15) that Paul is the messianic prophet who is to carry out the program of Isaiah 49:1-6: to deliver "light to the Gentiles."

By saying **now is the time,** Paul meant that the era that had been promised had arrived. In Jesus Christ, the **acceptable time** had arrived, and the offer of salvation was not to be taken lightly. Paul uses here for **time** the word *kairos,* which means the "divinely given opportunity." **Time** is not in the hands of men; it is ordained by God. Because time is in God's control, it is necessary for those who hear the message to realize the seriousness of God's once-for-all demand. Jerusalem did not recognize this divinely given opportunity when Jesus came to save it (Luke 19:44), and there can be no second chance. Thus Paul counsels the church to see the seriousness of God's offer of salvation and to recognize that God has granted the opportunity for obeying Christ. **Now** is while the gospel is being preached, the period before the end. With the coming of Jesus Christ, all of the prophecies of the Old Testament have been fulfilled (Mark 1:15), making **now** and "today" (Luke 4:21) important. **Now** is the period of grace which God has given in order for man to repent; for Paul it is urgent and not to be taken lightly.

³ We put no obstacle in any one's way, so that no fault
may be found with our ministry, ⁴ but as servants of God
we commend ourselves in every way: through great endurance, in afflictions, hardships, calamities,

---

The Hardship of Paul's Ministry, 6:3-13. [3] The connection of these verses with what precedes is not obvious.
Paul's point seems to be, after stating the content of the
gospel message (5:14-20) and the urgency of the moment
(6:1, 2), to defend himself against his opponents once
more. He wants to indicate to his detractors how seriously
he has taken his ministry. Thus he has put no **obstacle** in
anyone's way. The word here translated **obstacle** (*pro-
skopē*) means literally "an occasion for stumbling." It is
the image of placing something in someone's path which
makes him stumble (as in the word "stumbling block,"
Rom. 9:32f.). The Christian is never to place an **obstacle**
or "stumbling block" in the way of his brother (Rom.
14:13; 1 Cor. 8:9). Paul has lived with integrity in order
to prevent any **obstacle** from arising **so that no fault may
be found** with his **ministry.** Paul knows that if his integrity
is questionable, his entire ministry is also. Thus chapters
3—5 have defended his **ministry.** Now he defends his
ministry on personal grounds. The word for "find fault"
(*mōmaomai*) means also "to blame." One notices at 8:20
how careful Paul was to avoid any blame surrounding his
work. Not only does Paul live with integrity; he avoids
any false impression that would lead someone to **find
fault.**

[4] Paul returns here to the question of how the true
apostle commends himself. As we have seen (cf. comments
on 3:1; 4:2 and 5:12), Paul has been accused of commending himself (5:12); he has also said that his opponents commend themselves (3:1). Both Paul and his
opponents claim to be apostles (11:5). The claim to be a
valid apostle rests in large measure on how Paul and his
opponents **commend** themselves. The opponents commend
themselves by boasting of worldly things (11:16, 18), of
their advantages as Jews (11:22), and of their position as

⁵ **beatings, imprisonments, tumults, labors, watching, hunger;**

---

apostles (11:12). For Paul, the way they commend themselves invalidates their claim to authority.

The true apostle, according to Paul, must be like his master. Thus his power arises from his weakness and dependence on God (11:23ff.). The true apostle carries in his body the death of Jesus (4:10). Paul is therefore the legitimate apostle because he imitates the suffering and lowliness of Jesus. The long list which follows is Paul's claim to be a valid apostle. The catalogue is like a resumé of what is said at 11:23ff. In the Greek, each noun through the "power of God" in verse 7 follows the preposition *en*, literally "in." The KJV reflects this fact; the RSV does not. The first quality is **endurance** (*hupomonē*). **Endurance** is not coordinated with the nouns which follow. The term shows the attitude which allowed Paul to continue despite the deprivations listed in 4b, 5. The KJV regularly translates *hupomonē* as "patience," thus conveying the wrong impression. The word implies the ability to endure, despite the misfortunes. Paul's **afflictions** (*thlipseis*) have been vividly described at 1:8. **Hardships** are literally "necessities." The word *anagkē* also expresses a great need or distress, as when Jesus says (Luke 21:23) of the last days, "Great distress (hardships, *anagkē*) shall be upon the earth." **Hardships**, like **afflictions**, are therefore inevitable for the Christian (see notes on 1:8, 9). Paul has accepted them for the sake of Jesus. **Calamities** (*stenochōriais*) are literally "straits," pictured as a narrow place from which there is no escape. The verb form of the word is used at 6:12, and is translated "restricted." At 12:10, Paul says that he is content with such **calamities** for the sake of Christ.

[5] **Beatings** (*plēgai*) are mentioned also at 11:25. Acts records one such incident of a beating (16:22, 23). At 11:23, Paul says that the beatings were "countless." The word here also applies to wounds resulting from a beating. **Imprisonments** are mentioned also at 11:23,

⁶ **by purity, knowledge, forbearance, kindness, the Holy Spirit, genuine love,**

---

where Paul says "far more imprisonments." One may compare also the imprisonment recorded in Acts (16:23). These imprisonments come prior to Paul's imprisonments in Caesarea (Acts 24, 25) and Rome (Acts 28). Thus we have information which is not supplied in Acts. **Tumults** (*akatastasia*) in which Paul was involved are recorded throughout Acts in numerous riot scenes (Acts 13:50; 14:19; 17:5; 18:12; 19:29). The word signifies any kind of disorder. At 1 Corinthians 14:33, Paul says, "God is not a God of confusion (*akatastasia*), but of peace." At Luke 21:9, Jesus says that such **tumults** must take place before the end. Paul is concerned (2 Cor. 12:20) that upon returning to Corinth he may find such disorder (*akatastasia*). Paul's **labors**, not his worldly position, validate his apostleship. He is a better servant of Christ than his opponents because he has had "far greater labors" (11:23). The word **labors** (*kopos*) also implies "weariness" from labor. But for all who labor, Christ gives heavenly refreshment (Rev. 14:13; Matt. 11:28). **Watching** refers to sleepless nights (see 11:27) which are brought about by his concern for the churches. The word for **hunger** (*nēsteiai*) can mean either "fasting" or involuntary deprivation of food. In this context, Paul certainly is talking about a shortage of food (cf. Phil. 4:12; 2 Cor. 11:27).

[6] The list in this verse is not a continuation of the catalogue of misfortunes (from "afflictions" to "hunger"), but of the "endurance" in verse 4. Here we are informed of the reaction of Paul to adversity, enabling him to triumph despite these trials. **Purity** (*hagnotēs*) is an ideal for the Christian (cf. 1 John 3:3; James 3:17; 2 Cor. 11:2). In a narrower sense, the word means "chastity." Here Paul means "moral integrity." This is the meaning of the word at 7:11, where the RSV translates "guiltless." **Knowledge** of the gospel is meant here. Paul's ministry is a dissemination of the knowledge (2:14; 4:6; 10:5) of

⁷ truthful speech, and the power of God; with the weapons
of righteousness for the right hand and for the left;

God. This knowledge is not limited to factual information
only; it is a recognition of God and obedience to him.
Forbearance (*makrothumia*) is patient endurance of ill-
treatment without irritation or retaliation. This quality
is a Christian virtue throughout the New Testament
(Heb. 6:12; Gal. 5:22; Col. 3:12). The word is commonly
used of God's attitude toward men (Rom. 2:4; 9:22; 1
Peter 3:20). The **forbearance** of God, whereby he patiently
endures the sinfulness and rebelliousness of men, is reproduced in Paul's life. **Kindness** is also the attitude of
God and Christ (Eph. 2:7; Rom. 2:4). Therefore, a true
disciple will reproduce this quality in his life (Col. 3:12;
Gal. 5:22). Paul is able to withstand hardships through
the power supplied by the **Holy Spirit.** Although his opponents make claims for themselves, Paul's only claim is
the help of the **Holy Spirit.** His opponents may have advanced themselves by pretending to love. Paul has practiced **genuine love,** literally "unhypocritical" **love.** It is
this "unhypocritical love" that Paul has counseled the
Romans to practice (Rom. 12:9). The word that Paul
uses for **love** is *agapē*, which is unconquerable benevolence and good will. One who loves in this way is imitating God, who loved men while they were sinners
(Rom. 5:8; cf. Matt. 5:43-48).

[7] Paul's activities have been characterized by **truthful speech** (literally, "in a word of truth"). His opponents have said that he is "unskilled in speaking" (11:6)
and that his "speech is of no account" (10:10). The Corinthians seem to be unduly impressed by eloquence, as
Paul admits that his speech was not in "plausible words
of wisdom" (1 Cor. 2:4). Paul's defense is that he spoke
only the truth, i.e., the gospel. His message did not display his own eloquence; it displayed the power of God
(see 1 Cor. 1:24). If his own power had been on display,
their faith would have rested in men, and not in God.
The power of God is always evident in human weakness

⁸ in honor and dishonor, in ill repute and good repute.
We are treated as impostors, and yet are true; ⁹ as unknown,
and yet well known; as dying, and behold we live; as
punished, and yet not killed;

(12:11; 4:7), and thus Paul claims no power of his own.

Paul quite frequently describes Christian service in
terms of warfare. The word **weapons** (*hoplōn*) is thus
used figuratively for the instruments for good which the
Christian uses. At 10:4, Paul says that he is not equipped
with worldly weapons but with weapons of divine power.
Every Christian is to take up his **weapons,** and not use
his members as **weapons** of unrighteousness (Rom. 6:13;
cf. Rom. 13:12). Paul's weapon here is the defense which
righteousness provides. He is equipped with **the power
of God** (see 10:4). Therefore, he is equipped **for the
right hand and for the left,** i.e., for offense and defense.

[8] Paul takes up again here the adversities which
marked his ministry. The series of antitheses through
verse 10 dramatize both his affliction and his faithful endurance. They declare the difference between Paul's status before God and his status before men. Before men,
Paul has experienced **dishonor.** This **dishonor** (*atimia*)
Paul has experienced before the Corinthians because he
did not accept support from them (11:21). But in being
without honor among men, he still was only following
his Lord, for Jesus was without **honor** among men (Mark
6:4). The word **honor** (*doxa*) is the same word that is
translated "glory." He may have lost **honor** before men,
but not before God. The antithesis of **good repute** and
ill repute is the same as the one which precedes; **ill repute** refers to his outward reputation, and **good repute**
refers to his status before God. **We are treated** (RSV)
is not in the Greek; it is supplied to interpret Paul's meaning. To the world he is regarded as an **imposter,** yet before God he is **true** and sincere.

[9] Here, by new antitheses, Paul contrasts the visible
appearance with the essential reality. The carnal man has
been misled to think, because of Paul's sufferings, that

¹⁰ as sorrowful, yet always rejoicing; as poor, yet making many rich; as having nothing, and yet possessing everything.

¹¹ Our mouth is open to you, Corinthians; our heart is wide.

Paul is wrong. He seems to be **unknown,** or even rejected (*agnooumenoi*) by God, but in reality he is **known** by God. From a fleshly point of view he is **dying,** or constantly at the point of death; but from a spiritual point of view, he is alive (cf. 4:8-12; Ps. 118:17-18), having been "crucified with him" (Gal. 2:20). He seems to be **punished** or "chastened." The word for **punished** (*paideuein*) means here well-deserved punishment. It is the word for a father's just punishment of a child. Paul's thorn in the flesh (12:7) might look like **punishment** to the outsider. Yet God leaves room for rescue: **and yet not killed** (1:10; cf. 4:7-12).

[10] Paul's recent experience is one of being **sorrowful, yet always rejoicing.** He can rejoice in his sufferings (Col. 1:24). His sorrow is caused by the problems he faces with the churches; his joy comes when he sees them bear fruit (7:4ff.). The worldly man sees his poverty as a sign of disfavor; yet he can enrich the lives of men. In this also he is following his Lord, who became poor, "so that by his poverty you might become rich" (8:9). He has **nothing** in the way of position; yet these things do not count. He has counted them as "refuse" for the sake of knowing Jesus Christ (Phil. 3:8). In knowing Christ, he has **everything** (see 1 Cor. 3:22).

Verses 4-10 are intended to show how Paul commends himself. His commendation is that he has followed Jesus in taking up his cross, which validates his apostleship.

[11] After the long section on the apostolic ministry (2:17—6:10), Paul resumes the discussion of his relationships with the Corinthian church. He begins with an appeal for a warm return of the deep affection he has for them. This appeal, interrupted by a digression in 6:14—7:1, is completed in 7:2-4.

¹² You are not restricted by us, but you are restricted in
your own affections. ¹³ In return—I speak as to children—
widen your hearts also.

Paul's language in verses 9, 10 resembles Psalm 118:
17, 18. Now his message in vs. 11 is reminiscent of Psalm
119:32. The psalm says, "You enlarge my heart (or understanding)." Paul says, **Our heart is wide,** i.e., "You
have a large place in my heart." By analogy Paul says,
Our mouth is open to you, i.e., "We are speaking frankly
with you." If Paul's relationship with the Corinthians is
uneasy, Paul is **open** to them. He is prepared to be reconciled to them.

[12] Paul is "open" to them, but they are **restricted**
(closed) in their **affections.** Any barrier between them
is their own. The word for **affections** is *splagchnois.* It refers to the heart, liver, lungs, and intestines, regarded
as the seat of emotions.

[13] Paul pleads for them to remove any barrier to
affection. The expression **in turn** (*tēn de autēn antimis-
thian*) implies a service to be rendered in exchange for
another service. He has done his part; now they must do
their part. He speaks **as to children.** They are his **children**
in the faith, since he founded that church (cf. 1 Cor.
4:15; Gal. 4:19).

The Christian's Relation to Unbelievers, 6:14—7:1. In
the middle of Paul's defense of his ministry and his discussion of his relations to the Corinthian church, 6:14—
7:1 looks like a parenthesis. In this section Paul calls for
the church to separate itself from defiling influences.
Church consciousness always includes a consciousness of
separation and delimitation from the world. The church
is sanctified or "set apart" by God to fulfill God's service
(1 Cor. 1:2; Acts 20:32). The church is therefore to be
separated from all aspects of pagan worship (1 Cor. 10:1-
22) and from all that is immoral and sinful (1 Cor. 6:19).
The church finds separation from defiling influences to be
important in order to preserve its identity. The section at

¹⁴ Do not be mismated with unbelievers. For what partnership have righteousness and iniquity? Or what fellowship has light with darkness?

---

2 Corinthians 6:14—7:1 is an exhortation for the church to preserve its nature by separation from "unbelievers."

One may notice how neatly in the RSV 6:13 and 7:2 fit together when one omits 6:14—7:1. This fact, along with the apparent change of subject matter in 6:14—7:1, has caused a great number of biblical scholars to maintain that this section did not originally belong here. Furthermore, the subject matter of Paul's "previous letter," written before 1 Corinthians (cf. 1 Cor. 5:9), is the same as we encounter here (see Introduction). Consequently, it is believed by many that this passage is a part of the "lost letter" mentioned at 1 Corinthians 5:9. This explanation has certain difficulties, however. It does not tell us how such an insertion came to be placed here. New Testament letters were written on scrolls, and it would not have been easy to insert the material here. Further, it is not certain that this passage is out of place. Paul has been defending himself against troublesome opponents. It is plausible to suggest that the unbelievers of 6:14 are Paul's opponents and that he is exhorting them to draw lines of separation in order to preserve their identity as a faithful church.

[14] The entire section appears to be an elaboration of 14a: Do not be mismated with unbelievers. Mismated (*heterozugeō*) is literally, as the KJV translates, "unequally yoked." The word carries the idea of mating animals of different species (see Lev. 19:19, where the same word is used: "You shall not let your cattle breed with a different kind"). The idea of the "yoke" (see Deut. 22:10) is used figuratively several times in the New Testament (cf. 1 Tim. 6:1; Gal. 5:1; Acts 15:10). Jesus describes his way of life as a "yoke" (Matt. 11:29). The word was also used for a team of Jewish scholars sent on a mission. Thus Paul uses the word with reference to his ministry (1 Cor. 9:9; cf. Phil. 4:3; 1 Tim. 5:18). Here

in 6:14, the word **mismated** means "to live in the church with someone who does not share your presuppositions." Paul's admonition has been quoted by many to indicate that Paul is discussing the marriage relationship. The context forbids any such interpretation; no mention is made here of the marriage relationship. In addition, the Greek expression can best be translated, "Quit being mismated . . ." (which would be the opposite of the instructions in 1 Cor. 7:12f.). In this context Paul gives a call for separation from his opponents. The church loses its identity when it fails to separate itself from such influences, whether they are pagan (1 Cor. 10:1-22) or "pseudo-Christian."

The opponents are called **unbelievers** (*apistoi*). They have been blinded and deceived by Satan (4:4; 11:3; 13:3ff.). The word **unbelievers** is generally applied by Paul to pagans (1 Cor. 6:6; 7:12ff.; 10:27; 14:22ff.). Indeed, all of 6:14—7:1 could easily have been directed at pagan influences. Very likely, these are the kinds of exhortation Paul often used when there was a danger from idolatrous influences. What he has done is to take his usual argument against idolatry and apply it to his opponents.

A series of five questions, the first four of which are arranged in pairs, brings out how incongruous any bond is with those who do not share the presuppositions of the faithful. As Paul states the alternatives, the lines are clear: one can choose either **righteousness** or **iniquity.** There is for Paul no middle ground. The language that he uses (**light** and **darkness,** Belial, **righteousness** and **iniquity,** and the church as the temple) sounds very much like the language of the Qumran community which is reflected in the Dead Sea Scrolls. They too were concerned about hypocrites in their midst, and their leaders called for separation (Gärtner, p. 51). Paul here uses language that was familiar in this period of time to call for separation from his opponents.

At 14b, Paul implies that **righteousness** (*dikaiosunē*) and **unrighteousness** (*anomia*) have no **partnership** (*me-*

¹⁵ What accord has Christ with Belial? ' Or what has a believer in common with an unbeliever?
    ' Or *Beliar*

---

tochē). **Partnership** is here synonymous with **fellowship** in the next question (cf. 1 Cor. 10:16, 17). Both words mean "to share." **Righteousness** and **iniquity** are mutually exclusive; one cannot participate in both. In the same way, the church must choose between Paul and his opponents. **Light** and **darkness** are also mutually exclusive; one cannot have **fellowship** (*koinonia*, "to share," "to participate in") in both. Disciples are, according to Paul, "children of light" (Eph. 5:8) and "sons of light" (1 Thess. 5:5). Here the terms **light** and **darkness** distinguish the faithful from the unfaithful. Paul's opponents apparently called themselves "servants of light" (cf. 11:14; 4:6). Paul defends his own ministry against his opponents, since God's light has appeared to Paul (4:6). This distinction between "the sons of light" and "the sons of darkness" to divide mankind is found frequently in the Dead Sea Scrolls. There, as in 6:14, the "sons of light" are to separate themselves from the "sons of darkness" in their midst. By using these terms, Paul is using familiar language to encourage his readers to keep their identity by shutting out evil influences.

[15] The distinction is between **Christ** and **Belial**. **Belial** is referred to in the New Testament only here. The word is a compound of two Hebrew words, *bel* ("not") and *yal* ("useful"), and thus the word means literally "useless." The word is seldom used in the Old Testament, but it is used widely in late Jewish literature, especially in the Dead Sea Scrolls, in which **Belial** came to be the proper name for the prince of evil, Satan (cf. 11:3, 14). In the Dead Sea Scrolls, **Belial** is the one who leads the forces of evil in opposition to God. One of the writers of the Dead Sea Scrolls says (*War Scroll* 13:1-4), "Blessed be God . . . cursed be Belial." Here **Belial** is close in meaning to the "antichrist," who was expected before the end (1 John 2:18, 22; 2 John 7). "The Christian can

¹⁶ What agreement has the temple of God with idols?
For we are the temple of the living God; as God said,
   "I will live in them and move among them,
   and I will be their God,
   and they shall be my people.

---

share no more in the evil influences of Paul's opponents
than Christ can share in the nature of Satan," says Paul.

A **believer** and an **unbeliever** have nothing **in common** (*meris*). *Meris* here is literally translated "part" or
"portion." A Christian has a share of God's inheritance
(Col. 1:12); he has chosen the good "portion" (Luke 10:
42), and therefore he has nothing **in common** with Paul's
opponents. They do not "share" in the same things. Such
a difference calls for separation.

[16] **The temple of God** and **idols** were mutually exclusive; they never belonged together. Just as **idols** had
no place in **the temple of God,** enemies of the gospel
have no place in the church. Paul is not discussing literal
idols here. This seems to be an assured fact, especially
when we notice that the **temple** can hardly refer to the
Jerusalem temple. We do not find Paul faced with that
problem in 2 Corinthians, although in 1 Corinthians, idolatry was a problem. **Idols** were mentioned figuratively
in the Dead Sea Scrolls for any temptations to sin. That
use of **idols** is compatible with Paul's use here. **Idols** signifies any kind of evil.

That Paul is not talking about the Jerusalem **temple**
is confirmed by the statement, **we are the temple of the
living God.** The term **living God** was frequently used in
preaching to Gentiles (cf. 1 Thess. 1:9; Acts 14:15). This
description of God as the **living God** had developed in
Jewish circles where Jewish apologetics contrasted the
living God with lifeless idols (see the apocryphal addition to Daniel, Bel and the Dragon). The idea of the
church as God's temple occurs in 1 Corinthians 3:16, 17;
at 6:19 the individual Christian's body is God's temple
(cf. Eph. 2:21, 22). God's glory once resided at the Jerusalem temple in the holy of holies. Now God's glory

[17] Therefore come out from them,
and be separate from them, says the Lord,
and touch nothing unclean;
then I will welcome you,

---

has been removed from the temple and is to be found in the church. The church is the spiritual temple, and offers "spiritual sacrifices" (1 Peter 2:5).

The idea that the community is the **temple** is found nowhere in the Old Testament. This fact is not surprising since Israel made use of a literal temple. The Dead Sea Scrolls were written by a community which believed that those priests who led the temple worship were apostates. Consequently, they had no dealings with the actual temple. Instead, they spiritualized the concept of the temple, thus describing their community as God's temple. Thus when Paul describes the church as God's temple, he was spiritualizing the idea of the temple in the same way.

In 16b-18, Paul strings together a group of passages from the Old Testament. The purpose of these passages is: (a) to confirm that the church is God's temple, and therefore the place of God's presence; and (b) to give scriptural grounds for his exhortation that the temple should remain pure from defilement. Collections of Old Testament texts grouped around a theme are found elsewhere in the New Testament (see 1 Peter 2:6-8).

Verse 16b is a rather loose rendering of Ezekiel 37:27 and Leviticus 26:11, 12. The Old Testament passages cited indicate God's "presence" or "dwelling" in the tabernacle and temple. The words, "I will dwell among them," are quoted to show that God's presence or "dwelling" is now in the church. The idea of God's "dwelling" among his people is found elsewhere in the New Testament (John 14:23; 1:14; Rev. 21:3).

[17] The temple was always to remain pure. This section (6:14—7:1) is concerned with the purity of the church, God's temple. Paul paraphrases Isaiah 52:11 in order to justify his exhortation. The last line comes from Ezekiel 20:34. The passage in Isaiah concerns those who

¹⁸ and I will be a father to you,
and you shall be my sons and daughters,
says the Lord Almighty."
¹ Since we have these promises, beloved, let us cleanse ourselves from every defilement of body and spirit, and make holiness perfect in the fear of God.

---

incur ceremonial impurity. For Paul, the passage concerns those who are made impure by the defiling elements in the church. God's demand is followed by a promise. The last line of 17, followed by verse 18, gives the promise of God to all those who comply with God's demand for separation. Here God will **welcome** those who comply with him.

[18] Paul quotes here the second promise, which comes from 2 Samuel 7:14. It is natural that Paul should quote this passage when discussing the temple. The passage Paul quotes says, "I will be his father, and he shall be my son." The promise follows after God's promise to David to provide the temple for him (2 Sam. 7:10ff.). Paul quotes the passage to say that the promise remains good. The heir of this promise at 2 Samuel 7:14 is the church, God's new temple. This passage is cited quite frequently in the Dead Sea Scrolls, indicating that the Qumran community considered itself heir to this promise also.

Paul adds **and daughters** to his quotation of 2 Samuel 7:14. Perhaps he is thinking of such a passage as Isaiah 43:6. Perhaps he is led to make this addition by the special prominence of women in the Corinthian church (cf. 1 Cor. 7).

[1] These **promises** are so assuring that they should motivate Paul's readers to action. Since the temple must be pure, the church, as the true temple, is told, **let us cleanse ourselves of every defilement of body and spirit.** The Jerusalem temple had to maintain its purity or cleanliness before God. The word here for **cleanse,** *katharizein,* was also used of ritual cleansing required for the temple service. The defilements are of **body** (literally

² Open your hearts to us; we have wronged no one, we have corrupted no one, we have taken advantage of no one.

"flesh") and spirit (*pneuma*). It is doubtful that Paul has in mind two separate categories of defilements. Body and spirit make up the whole man (see 1 Thess. 5:23). Holiness (*hagiōsunē*) is a quality that is attributed to every Christian as a result of his acceptance of Christ at baptism (see 1 Cor. 6:11). The word implies separation from defilement and a cleansing. This sanctification is the activity of the Holy Spirit (2 Thess. 2:13; 1 Peter 1:2). The Christian has already been set apart for Christ, and is therefore a saint (see 1 Cor. 1:2). This process of becoming holy is not completed yet; the process is completed or made perfect when one has completely cleansed himself of corrupting influences.

Paul's Relation to the Corinthian Church, 7:2-16. [2] At 7:2, Paul returns to a more immediate discussion of his relations with the Corinthian church. He now returns to a greater appeal for affection from his readers that he had begun in 6:11-13 and completes what he had to say. One may notice that 6:13b and 7:2a seem to say the same thing. In the RSV, 6:13b says, "widen your hearts," while 7:2a says, **Open your hearts.** Although Paul is calling for reconciliation in both statements, the linguistic similarities are not so striking in Greek. Paul says literally in 7:2, "Make room for us," to which we must add for clarification, "in your hearts," or "in your minds."

Reconciliation between the Corinthians and Paul is hardly possible as long as they continue to listen to false charges made against Paul. Thus Paul emphatically denies such slanders. At 7:12, Paul refers to someone in the Corinthian church "who did the wrong"; this person seems to have led a rebellion against Paul. Paul may be contrasting himself to the offender. Paul has **wronged no one.** He has **corrupted** (*ephtheiramen*) **no one.** The word can either mean "to corrupt by misleading tactics" or "to ruin financially." In view of Paul's concern over

³ I do not say this to condemn you, for I said before that you are in our hearts, to die together and to live together. ⁴ I have great confidence in you; I have great pride in you; I am filled with comfort. With all our affliction, I am overjoyed.

---

the collection (chs. 8—9) and his defense of his behavior at 11:20, he may be defending himself against the charge that he misused money. He has **taken advantage** (*pleonektein*) of no one. Here also he is answering a charge made against him. At 12:17, he answers the same charge. The word there certainly suggests that Paul has been charged with **taking** financial **advantage** of the church.

[3] Since verse 2 may be an allusion to persons who conducted themselves improperly, Paul does not wish to leave the impression that he wants to reopen the conflict. Therefore, he says, **I do not say this to condemn you.** At 6:11, Paul said, "Our heart is wide." Now he says, **you are in our hearts.** It is not certain what Paul is referring to when he says, **I said before.** These exact words have not been said. Yet he has indicated his affection for them previously, and he is very likely referring to a previous statement of his affection for them (see 6:11). The bonds of fellowship are so intense that they can **die together** and **live together.** The divisions Paul has discussed at length have no place because the church is a fellowship. "No one lives to himself or dies to himself" (Rom. 14:7). They have died together by sharing in the death of Christ (5:14), and they **live together** by no longer living for themselves (5:15); now they live for Christ. This fellowship is too great to be destroyed by divisions.

[4] Verse 4 is filled with exultation which recent events have caused. His **confidence** (*parrēsia*) in them is **great.** This **confidence** is based on the right disposition of his heart to them. The word is used here almost in the sense of "affection." **Great** also is his **pride.** *Kauchēma*, translated here **pride,** is usually translated "boast." Self-boasting is precluded by the fact that one is not saved by meritorious works. However, Paul does at times boast

⁵ For even when we came into Macedonia, our bodies
had no rest but we were afflicted at every turn—fighting
without and fear within.

---

of what Christ does through him (Rom. 15:17f.; 1 Cor.
15:10; cf. also the comments on 1:14). Thus it is not
uncommon for Paul to "boast" or have **pride** in the
strength of a congregation which he has founded, as he
does here (cf. 8:24; 9:2f.). Paul's opponents are boastful,
but in boasting they only commend themselves (3:1;
5:12). Paul boasts of others. He is **filled with comfort,** having received the good news from Titus of their repentance (7:6). This **comfort** came from God, according to
7:6, and Titus merely served as God's agent in bringing
comfort to him. It is this experience of God's **comfort**
that has caused Paul to give the sublime teaching at
1:3ff. on the **comfort** which God always gives in affliction.
He is **overjoyed** (literally, "I abound with joy beyond
measure") in **affliction** (*thlipsis*). This **affliction** is described at 7:5 as "fighting without and fear within." That
was his condition before Titus brought the good news.
The news from Titus turned his **affliction** to joy, which en-
ables Paul to say at 1:5; "As we share in Christ's sufferings,
so through Christ do we share in comfort too."

[5] In 2:12, 13, Paul was ready to tell how Titus met
him in Macedonia with good news from Corinth. He
turned aside, however, to thank God for his place in the
ministry and went on to discuss at length the nature of
his ministry. One may notice here that 2:13 and 7:5 fit
to form a complete narrative; 2:14 to 7:4 form an extended parenthesis. Only now does he resume the story
of Titus' coming. But he was already thinking of it in
verse 4, which reflects the comfort and joy which Paul
experienced. Paul had agreed with Titus previously to
meet him on his return back from Corinth, and Paul had
gone to **Macedonia** to meet him. His condition there was
difficult: **Our bodies had no rest.** The word for bodies
here (*sarx*) is literally "flesh." As the next phrase indicates, body or "flesh" means the whole person. The same

101

⁶ But God, who comforts the downcast, comforted us by the coming of Titus, ⁷ and not only by his coming but also by the comfort with which he was comforted in you, as he told us of your longing, your mourning, your zeal for me, so that I rejoiced still more. ⁸ For even if I made you sorry with my letter, I do not regret it (though I did regret it), for I see that that letter grieved you, though only for a while.

---

meaning is found at 2:13, where Paul says, "My mind could not find rest." The **fighting** may have included physical threats against Paul made by pagan foes (cf. Acts 16:23; 17:5; Phil. 1:30). **Within** was fear (*phobos*), probably anxiety over the news he was to hear from Titus.

[6] But in the midst of Paul's anxiety, Titus brought him **comfort**. This **comfort** is a part of the abundant comfort that Paul always finds in his affliction (cf. 1:3-6; 7:13). Such an experience causes Paul to say that **God** always **comforts the downcast**. This picture of God as comforter is found also in Isaiah 49:13. The word for **coming** (*parousia*) is often used elsewhere in the New Testament for the "advent" of Christ at the end of the age.

[7] Evidently Titus had been in low spirits before going to Corinth; probably he had little hope that his mission would be successful, knowing what bitterness Paul had experienced there (see 2:1). Thus the repentance of the Corinthians had been a **comfort** to him, as it had been to Paul. The joy that Titus felt was so great and so contagious that it doubled the joy of Paul; he **rejoiced still more**. Titus told of their **longing** (*epipothēsis*) to see Paul. This **longing** of theirs is mentioned again at verse 11. **Mourning** (*odurmos*) is a feeling of bitter remorse (see Matt. 2:18). Paul's "tearful letter" (2:4) had aroused them to remorse over their actions. Titus told also of their **zeal** for Paul. *Zēlos* can mean "jealousy" (see 11:2) or "zeal," as here. The word indicates a passionate state of mind. Paul is gratified to know that the Corinthians still have deep feelings for him.

[8] At 2:4, Paul refers to the letter he wrote "with

⁹ As it is, I rejoice, not because you were grieved, but because you were grieved into repenting; for you felt a godly grief, so that you suffered no loss through us.

tears." The letter also occasioned grief with its recipients, the Corinthians. Perhaps Paul does not want the Corinthians to think that he is exulting in their humiliation. Thus he gives here the reason for his joy. Things have worked out well, and his pain has turned to joy. Paul did, however, experience considerable remorse in sending the tearful letter to Corinth (**though I did regret it**). But he considered the pain necessary in order to bring about a change of heart among the Corinthians. Paul's expression, **made you sorry** (or "caused you grief"), does not imply repentance. It implies only a deep regret. The purpose of this regret was to lead them to repentance. The sorrow or grief (*lupē*) was only temporary; the purpose of Paul's letter was not to cause grief, but to awaken the Corinthians to their past sin.

[9] Now that the Corinthians have completely changed their attitude and Paul has learned of it, he can rejoice, as verses 4, 7 have said he does. That they **were grieved** gives him no joy; he regrets the necessity of that. Sorrow in some cases can serve no useful purpose; it can cause the grieving one to "be overwhelmed with excessive sorrow" (2:7), so much that the person gives up his faith. On the other hand, sorrow can lead to repentance, as it did with the Corinthians. The difference is that their sorrow is **godly** (*kata theon*). This is the grief that leads to repentance. To have **godly grief** is not to be sorry for the consequences of one's actions; it is to realize that one's offense is against God. The Corinthians were aware that their wrong had been not merely against Paul, but also against God.

The correct kind of grief leads to repentance (*metanoia*). Repentance is a rare word in Paul's writings, and the verb "repent" occurs only once (12:21). The word has the fundamental meaning of a "change of mind." It is to be distinguished from the word "regret" or "remorse"

103

¹⁰ For godly grief produces a repentance that leads to salvation and brings no regret, but worldly grief produces death.

(*metamelesthai*) in verse 8. In verse 10 Paul speaks of a repentance without regret. Regret can often carry simply the meaning of the natural result of an imprudent action, whereas repentance is directed toward a reorientation of one's life toward God. This distinction between repentance and regret is useful, although the words may merge in meaning in a few instances. Repentance is the change of thought and will which releases one from evil. It suggests that one comes to a different view of something. Thus for Paul, the right kind of grief does not stop with remorse and contrition; it leads to a complete change of behavior, a reorientation of the will toward God.

Godly grief, says Paul, has saved the Corinthians from **loss** (literally, "in nothing you suffered loss from us"). What does Paul mean by "suffer loss" (*zēmiōthēnai*)? The word for suffer loss is used in 1 Corinthians 3:15 for the loss of one's reward (cf. Phil. 3:7). According to 1 Corinthians 3:14, if the apostle's work survives until the end, he will receive a reward. If his work does not survive (1 Cor. 3:15), it will be a **loss** to him. Paul is responsible, according to verse 10, for the salvation of the Corinthian church. Thus any action which alienates the Corinthians, such as a letter written too hastily, might cause them to suffer loss because of him. Paul, feeling a tremendous responsibility, wants to maintain cordial relations.

[10] The "loss" of verse 9 would have occurred if their grief had been **worldly grief.** To say that **worldly grief** produces **death** is to repeat Paul's concern in verse 9, the fear that they might suffer loss. **Worldly grief** might have caused a remorse that ended only in bitterness and death, as in the case of Judas (Matt. 27:3-5). **Death** here does not indicate that immediate physical death follows "worldly grief." **Death** stands here for the complete alienation from God which leaves one without hope for future fellowship with God (cf. Gal. 5:21; 1 Cor. 6:9, 10). It is the opposite

104

¹¹ For see what earnestness this godly grief has produced
in you, what eagerness to clear yourselves, what indignation, what alarm, what longing, what zeal, what punishment! At every point you have proved yourselves guiltless
in the matter. ¹² So although I wrote to you, it was not on
account of the one who did the wrong, nor on account of
the one who suffered the wrong, but in order that your
zeal for us might be revealed to you in the sight of God.

---

of salvation (*sotēria*). Since this repentance leads to salvation, there is no regret. Here again, as in verses 8-9, Paul
makes a distinction between repentance and regret. Repentance is directed toward God and leads to salvation.

[11] At 7:11, Paul comments on the signs that the repentance of the Corinthians was genuine. The genuineness
of their repentance is judged by its results. Paul uses seven
words to emphasize the commendable attitude of the
Corinthians. The earnestness which they have displayed
indicates a willingness to make every effort to remedy the
situation at Corinth (see 8:16, where the word is used
again); their attempts to comply with Paul are not half-
hearted. They have wanted to clear themselves or "make
a defense" (*apologia*). The word means literally "to give a
defense," as in court (cf. Acts 22:1; 2 Tim. 4:16). Here
they will clear themselves by their compliance with Paul's
demands. Indignation is also "anger"; probably their indignation is directed at the chief troublemaker (2:5). They
experienced fear of the indignation of Paul; there was
longing (see vs. 7) for a resumption of a good relationship
with Paul and a zeal to do away with the one who had
offended Paul (2:5); thus their zeal took the form of
punishment. The punishment appears to be expulsion from
the church. At every point they have proved themselves
guiltless, or "innocent" (*hagnos*). The same word is used
at 11:2 in the sense of a "chaste virgin." Their dedication
has been above criticism; they did not equivocate in
complying with Paul's demands.

[12] This verse is reminiscent of 2:9. Paul says there
that his purpose in writing the painful letter was to test

¹³ **Therefore we are comforted.**

And besides our own comfort we rejoiced still more at the joy of Titus, because his mind has been set at rest by you all. ¹⁴ For if I have expressed to him some pride in you, I was not put to shame; but just as everything we said to you was true, so our boasting before Titus has proved true.

---

their obedience. It seems unlikely that Paul wrote with little concern for the one who **did the wrong** or the one who **suffered the wrong**, as the translation may suggest. As 2:5 indicates, Paul had immense concern over this problem.

The one who did wrong is mentioned at 2:5-11. **The one who suffered wrong** is very likely Paul himself, or at least one of Paul's messengers. In some way Paul's leadership had been challenged; it was a crisis that could be resolved only when the Corinthians showed their **zeal for** him. He had no interest in retaliation, as 2:5-11 shows. It is not certain what role the false teachers played here. The issue here appears to be more a personal insult to Paul than a doctrinal issue.

[13] **Therefore** refers obviously to the zeal or dedication they have shown toward Paul; this zeal is the source of Paul's **comfort.** As verse 6 and 1:3, 4 show, the **comfort** comes from God. Because Paul's concern is so closely involved with Titus' concerns, Paul rejoiced at Titus' joy. The church, because it is a fellowship, shares together in its sorrows and its comforts (1:7). Probably Titus feared unhappy circumstances, but their zeal set **his mind at rest** (literally, "his spirit was refreshed"). Paul relates in 2:13 that, before seeing Titus, his "mind could not find rest." Now that Titus has his mind **at rest,** Paul shares in this joy.

[14] After such sordid conditions as Paul experienced on his last visit to Corinth, it may be surprising that Paul has expressed any **pride** in the Corinthians. Paul often boasted of the qualities of his churches (see comments on 7:4). Thus before Titus left for Corinth, Paul expressed his **pride** (*kauchēsis*, "boasting") in them. That they have not brought shame is more grounds for Paul's great joy. His

¹⁵ **And his heart goes out all the more to you, as he remembers the obedience of you all, and the fear and trembling
with which you received him.** ¹⁶ **I rejoice, because I have
perfect confidence in you.**

love for them had enabled him to see beyond that moment
of distress, and to say good things about them.

[15] According to 2:9, their obedience was tested by
Paul's letter. Here they survived the test. Titus remembers well the deference they gave him. Thus his **heart**
(*splagchna*, "emotions") is very much with them. They
had received him **with fear and trembling.** The same expression is used in 1 Corinthians 2:3 of Paul's manner of
preaching. It implies humility. The Corinthians had given
up the arrogance they had displayed on Paul's previous
visit.

[16] Paul again stresses his joy, provoked by his **confidence** which he has in them. His **confidence** has proved to
be well founded. *Tharrō,* translated here **confidence,** is
literally, "I am bold to you." He may here be answering
charges made against him that he lacks boldness, since at
10:1, 2 his opponents are charging him with not being
"bold" in the presence of the church. Here his boldness is
grounded in their good behavior.

THE COLLECTION, 8—9

The Liberality of the Macedonians, 8:1-15

Chapters 8 and 9 form a distinct section of the epistle.
This discussion of the collection of funds for the church
is discussed at great length only here in New Testament
writings. Paul had mentioned in 1 Corinthians 16:1, 2 a
collection which was to be taken to Jerusalem. Although
almost a year had passed since Paul had encouraged them
to contribute to the collection (see 8:10), Paul finds it
necessary to encourage the church to complete it. Probably the troubles at Corinth had hindered any progress on
the collection. According to 11:7-11 and 12:16-18, Paul's

107

opponents had criticized Paul for his part in the collection for personal profit. The fact that Paul finds it necessary
to argue the point with his extended discussion here,
whereas he only mentions the collection at 1 Corinthians
16:1, indicates that serious questions have been raised. Although he has been reconciled to them, he still wishes to
answer any doubts that have been raised about the collection.

According to Galatians 2:1-10, a working agreement was
reached between the Gentile churches, represented by
Paul, and the Jewish churches, represented by Peter,
James and John. The arrangement whereby they could
cooperate was cemented by Paul's agreement to "remember the poor" (Gal. 2:10)—a promise Paul was "eager" to
fulfill. The "poor" were probably the poverty-striken Christians in Jerusalem. No doubt the Jerusalem church con-
sisted largely of the poor (see Acts 11:29, although the
reference there probably refers to an earlier collection).
A large part of Paul's third missionary journey seems to
have been devoted to organizing and winding up the collection. Participating in the collection were the churches of
Galatia (1 Cor. 16:1), Macedonia (2 Cor. 8:1), and
Corinth, representing every field in which Paul had worked.

Obviously, Paul's purpose in being concerned about
the collection was to relieve the poor saints in Jerusalem.
But there was another reason for Paul's interest in the collection. He saw here an opportunity to solve the problem
that had earlier brought him to Jerusalem (Gal. 2:10).
The collection served as a "peace offering" to unify the
Jewish and Gentile Churches. Paul asks for the prayers of
the church in Rome, that his service "may be acceptable
to the saints" (Rom. 15:31). He gives as further reason
for the collection the principle that the Gentiles, having
received spiritual blessings from the Jewish Christians in
Jerusalem, should reciprocate with material blessings (Rom.
15:26f.; Gal. 6:6; 2 Cor. 8:13f.). This aim of unifying the
churches explains Paul's great sense of obligation to complete the collection and to deliver it to Jerusalem. That
Paul does not participate in this collection solely for the

¹ **We want you to know, brethren, about the grace of God which has been shown in the churches of Macedonia,**

---

sake of relieving poverty can also be seen in the pace with which Paul gathered the funds. The collection is first mentioned in Galatians, written around A.D. 53. It is mentioned as still being in progress in Romans, which was written not earlier than A.D. 56. Thus it was several years before Paul completed the collection.

[1] Paul begins by pointing to the good example of the churches of Macedonia. Apparently, the Corinthians had shown a keen interest in the collection from the first, about which Paul boasted to the Macedonians (9:2). In the intervening period, however, troubles at Corinth had halted any progress on the collection. During this time, as verse 1 shows, the Macedonians had gone on with the collection. Now Paul wishes to stimulate in the Corinthians the zeal they had originally shown in order that Paul will not be embarrassed by the Corinthians after boasting about them. **Macedonia** would include such towns as Philippi, Berea, and Thessalonica. Paul does not specify which towns are involved. When discussing the collection, he seems to prefer to name geographical districts, not towns or congregations. Thus he names "the churches of Galatia" (1 Cor. 16:1) and "Achaia" (2 Cor. 9:2), of which Corinth was the chief city (cf. 1:1).

Only in 2 Corinthians 8 and 9 is the collection referred to as a **grace**. Elsewhere it is referred to as a contribution (*logeia,* 16:1), as "aid" (Rom. 15:25; *diakonōn,* "serving"), and as a "fellowship" (Rom. 15:26). The word **grace** here suggests that the collection is not the product of human effort; the collection results from nothing less than the grace of God. *Charis,* **grace,** is used consistently in chapters 8 and 9 for the collection. At 8:6, 7, 19, the word is translated "gracious work;" at 8:4, it is translated as "favor."

How can Paul regard participation in the collection as **grace** (*charis*)? **Grace** means primarily "favor," "good will," or "an undeserved gift." **The grace of God** usually

² for in a severe test of affliction, their abundance of joy and their extreme poverty have overflowed in a wealth of liberality on their part. ³ For they gave according to their means, as I can testify, and beyond their means, of their own free will,

---

refers to God's free gift of salvation in Jesus Christ. This free gift is alluded to in 8:9 as the "grace of our Lord Jesus." The church has an opportunity to participate in God's **grace** by imitating Jesus' sacrifice. This grace is **shown** (literally "given") in the church when God creates the conditions for sharing in his **grace.**

[2] Verses 2, 3 indicate how the Macedonians imitated or participated in God's grace. Just as Jesus "became poor for our sakes" (8:9), they gave out of **extreme poverty** (literally, "down to the depth poverty"). It is useless here to speculate what caused the **extreme poverty.** Early churches generally came from the lowest social strata, and thus poverty was never uncommon (see 1 Cor. 1:26-28). There was also **a severe test of affliction.** The **affliction** was probably ill-treatment from nonchristians (1 Thess. 1:6; 2:14). The **affliction** Paul experienced in Macedonia may have been from the same sources (see 7:5). There are two main contrasts in this verse: (a) between heavy **affliction** and abundant **joy** (see 7:4), and (b) between **extreme poverty** and a **wealth of liberality.** Paul himself frequently experienced **joy** in the midst of affliction, since Christian joy does not depend on outward circumstances (see Col. 1:24). The word for **liberality** is literally, "with singleness of aim." **Liberality** results when one has that singleness of motive (see 9:11, 13, where the same word is used). Their **liberality** must have been evident in the size of their contribution.

[3] The Macedonians have given not merely **according to their means** (*kata dunamin*), i.e., what one would expect from good Christians. They had no surplus from which to contribute, as verse 2 shows. They gave **beyond their means** (*para dunamin*). *Dunamis* is used mostly in the sense of "power" (cf. 12:9, 4:7). The word also conveys the

⁴ begging us earnestly for the favor of taking part in the relief of the saints—

---

sense of "ability" or "means," as it does here. Their giving needed in no way to be coerced; it was of their own free will (*authairetoi*). That the Corinthians should also give without "compulsion" is indicated at 9:7. Paul does not seem to have needed to employ tactics of coercion. He has already impressed on the minds of the Corinthians the importance of the collection for unifying Gentile and Jewish churches.

[4] The verse says literally, "with much exhortation begging of us the grace and the fellowship of the saints." Since Paul is the leader and organizer of the collection, the Macedonians hear about this service and beg Paul for the privilege of participating in it. The word translated **favor** (*charis*) is the word which is usually translated here "gracious work." This grace, which was exemplified by Jesus' gift of himself (8:9), is imitated by Christians. The Macedonians beg to be able to participate in an act of grace.

The collection is also a fellowship. *Koinōnia*, translated here **taking part,** is an important New Testament word. The word signifies a relationship of sharing. It is most often translated "fellowship," a word which signifies this sharing. The extent of this fellowship is seen where Paul discusses the collection in Romans 15:27: "for if the Gentiles have come to share in (or "have fellowship in") their spiritual blessings, they ought also to be of service to them in material blessings." This fellowship of Christians is an experience which is found in the Lord's Supper (1 Cor. 10:16). Fellowship is also evident in the collection (see Rom. 12:13). The collection is therefore not merely a financial matter. It expresses symbolically the union between Jewish and Gentile churches.

The word **relief** is literally "ministry" (*diakonia*) or "service." The same word is used for the collection at 9:1, 12 (cf. Acts 11:29; 12:25). For Paul, the collection was not what "charity" implies in modern speech; the collec-

[5] and this, not as we expected, but first they gave themselves to the Lord and to us by the will of God. [6] Accordingly we have urged Titus that as he had already made a beginning, he should also complete among you this gracious work.

---

tion was a "ministry" of love, a "service" performed because of one's relationship to Jesus Christ, the true Servant.

Saints (*hagioi*) means "sanctified" or "set apart" for God's service, and so the word applies to all Christians. Here Paul has in mind the poor of Jerusalem.

[5] The service of the Macedonians was not what Paul **expected,** but in a spirit that went beyond what was anticipated. Paul has said at 5:15 the death of Christ means that Christians should "live no longer for themselves but for him. . . ." The Macedonians have followed that ideal. They **gave themselves to the Lord.** The giving of money followed the giving of their lives to Christ. Their sacrificial giving symbolized that their lives were already given to him. When they **gave themselves** sacrificially to God, it was his **will** that they give themselves to Paul's work.

[6] In verses 1-5 the example of the Macedonian churches has been presented as a challenge to the Corinthians. Paul has been so inspired by the success of the collection at Macedonia that he is given determination that he will be successful here also. So great is his hope that he has already boasted to Titus about them (7:4; 9:3). According to 1 Corinthians 16:1-4; 2 Corinthians 8:10, the **beginning** was a considerable time in the past. The **beginning** plans had been interrupted by troubles at Corinth. Now Titus, who has recently returned from Corinth, will return there to **complete this gracious work** or "grace" (*charis*). It is a **gracious work** in response to the grace of God (see 8:9). Since Paul never refers in chapters 8 and 9 to the "collection," as in 16:1, it is possible that he is speaking of the collection in the highest possible terms to avoid a commercial connotation. Criticisms of his ministry have very likely caused Paul to avoid commercial language.

⁷ Now as you excel in everything—in faith, in utterance, in knowledge, in all earnestness, and in your love for us— see that you excel in this gracious work also.

⁸ I say this not as a command, but to prove by the earnestness of others that your love also is genuine. ⁹ For you know the grace of our Lord Jesus Christ, that though he was rich, yet for your sake he became poor, so that by his poverty you might become rich.

---

[7] The Corinthians are a gifted church; they **excel in everything**. Paul has mentioned in 7:11 the areas in which the church has excelled. No other mention is made in 2 Corinthians of their abundance of **faith**; he does hope in 10:15 that their **faith** will increase. At 1 Corinthians 1:4, Paul praised their gift of **utterance** or "speech." If they were especially qualified in speaking, one may see here why they seemed to be sensitive to Paul's inability of "speech" (10:10; 11:6). Their **knowledge** is also praised in 1 Corinthians 8:1ff., where Paul counsels them against the abuse of such knowledge. Here Paul speaks favorably of their **knowledge**. The **earnestness** (*spoudē*) or enthusiasm for doing right has already been mentioned (see 7:11). Their recent repentence has confirmed their **love** for Paul. Literally, he says, "the love in you which is from us," i.e., the love which is in you which we inspired in you by our concern for you. Now his concern is that they abound in responding to God's grace by participating in this grace (**gracious work**). They must **excel** or "overflow." Just as God overflows in his goodness, they must **excel** in their response to God.

[8] Just as the Macedonians gave voluntarily (vs. 3), Paul does not give a **command** (*epitagē*) to the Corinthians. His instruction comes in the form of **advice** (vs. 10). His instruction is reminiscent of 1 Corinthians 7:6, 25, where Paul refrains from commanding. He does not "lord it over" anyone's faith (1:24). He does, however, have a strong way of encouraging them. He wishes to **prove** (or "test") the genuineness of their love.

[9] In order to stimulate the Corinthians to this **gracious**

¹⁰ **And in this matter I give my advice: it is best for you now to complete what a year ago you began not only to do but to desire,**

---

work, Paul recalls the greatest example of **grace.** The knowledge of the **grace of our Lord Jesus Christ** should stimulate the Corinthians to respond to this **grace** by their own act of **grace.** They **know** this **grace** because it has been the subject of Paul's preaching. He himself was the recipient of God's **grace.** Christ was **rich** (*plousios*) in his preexistent state. He was, according to Philippians 2:6, in "the form of God." **Yet for your sake he became poor** (*eptōcheusen*). This saying is equivalent to the saying in Philippians 2:7, "He emptied himself." The poverty referred to here was the poverty of the human condition, the poverty of being subject to suffering and death. Paul thinks here of the "Son of man," who had "no place to lay his head" (Matt. 8:20). The purpose of his **grace was that you might become rich.** Only through this poverty, i.e., his death, is fellowship with God restored (see 5:21). Paul's opponents, who know Jesus "from a human point of view" (literally "according to the flesh," 5:16), have put no emphasis on the saving importance of Christ's death. Paul affirms here that this **grace** is at the center of the Christian faith.

Very few passages discuss the preexistence of Christ in the New Testament. The reason for this fact is probably that the New Testament is more concerned with the significance of Christ's death and resurrection. Yet we may notice several passages in which the New Testament affirms the preexistence of Christ. Paul says that Christ was in the "form of God" (Phil. 2:6), and that the world was "created through him" (Col. 1:16). The Gospel of John says that he was "in the beginning" with God (John 1:1), and that he once said of himself, "Before Abraham was, I am" (John 8:58). The writer of Hebrews said (1:2) that through him God "created the world" (cf. Prov. 8:22).

[10] The giving of **advice** (*gnōmē*) is reminiscent of

114

¹¹ so that your readiness in desiring it may be matched by your completing it out of what you have. ¹² For if the readiness is there, it is acceptable according to what a man has, not according to what he has not.

---

1 Corinthians 7:25, where Paul advises, but does not command, concerning the behavior of the "unmarried." **It is best for you** is better translated, as it is in the KJV, "it is expedient for you." The idea had originally been enthusiastically accepted by them; now it would be good for them to pursue it. To stop would be demoralizing for them. **A year ago** (*apo perusi*) also means "last year." An entire year had not elapsed since the project had been initiated, but a new year had come. They did not begin the project begrudgingly because of Paul's influence; it had been their **desire.** Very likely, false teachers had a discouraging effect on their **desire** to **complete** the task, causing Paul to remind them that they once were enthusiastic about the project.

[11] The earlier **readiness** (*prothumia*), about which Paul has boasted to Titus (9:2), must be matched by completion of the task. The RSV here obscures what is in Greek an emphatic "now" (*nuni de*). Enough time has elapsed. Now is the time to complete what was begun long ago. The new point added in this verse and the next is that the giving is to be according to ability. They should complete the collection **out of what** they **have.** He is not asking them to give, as the Macedonians did, "beyond their means" (vs. 3). He asks only that they give according to their ability.

[12] This verse is reminiscent of the poor widow at Mark 12:43, "who put more into the treasury" than anyone else. The **readiness** is what counts. Their earlier **readiness,** which may have been undermined by Paul's opponents, must be restored. Paul's statement sounds like a response to people who were claiming the inability to pay.

[13] I do not mean that others should be eased and you burdened, [14] but that as a matter of equality your abundance at the present time should supply their want, so that their abundance may supply your want, that there may be equality. [15] As it is written, "He who gathered much had nothing over, and he who gathered little had no lack."

[13,14] It is not unlikely that Paul in verse 13 is answering charges made by Paul's opponents, especially if his opponents are anti-Jerusalem (as some suggest). An opponent could have represented the collection as a Jewish attempt to make financial gain off the Greek churches, and thus an attempt to place a burden on the Corinthians (see 12:16-18). Paul answers that such a charge is absurd. The point is to achieve **equality,** which is mentioned twice in verse 14. This **equality** in external matters was characteristic of the earliest church, described in Acts (2:44f.; 4:36). This **equality** is stated in a different way where the collection is discussed in Romans 15:27. There it is achieved when the Gentile churches contribute material things in response to the spiritual blessings they have received from the Jews. Since Christianity is largely a fellowship of sharing (*koinōnia*), the sharing of goods can be a demonstration of the **equality** of Christians with each other.

Verse 14 emphasizes the Corinthians' **abundance at the present time.** The suggestion is that at a future time, circumstances will cause them to be receiving aid from the Judean churches. In view of the chronic poverty of the Jerusalem churches, this possibility seems to be only theoretical.

Your abundance indicates that, although the Corinthians came from the lower economic and social classes (1 Cor. 1:26), they were better off than most Christians. They can be contrasted here to the Macedonians (vss. 1, 2), who knew great poverty.

[15] Paul quotes here from Exodus 16:18. The passage does not mention giving to those who are in need, but only the statement that no matter how much manna any Israelite

¹⁶ But thanks be to God who puts the same earnest
care for you into the heart of Titus. ¹⁷ For he not only
accepted our appeal, but being himself very earnest he is
going to you of his own accord.

---

gathered, he had just enough. Paul uses that passage to
show a biblical basis for economic equality among Christians.

The Recommendation of Titus, 8:16-24

[16] Beginning with verse 16, Paul gives the credentials
of the three messengers who were to complete the collection. He adopts this method not only to keep critics from
accusing him of making financial profit from the collection
but also, as 9:3-5 suggests, because he has told Macedonia
that Corinth has the collection ready, and he wants it to
be complete before he and his Macedonian companions
arrive. This section (16-24) connects with verse 6 and
completes what Paul there started to say; verses 7-15 interrupted the details of how the collection was to be completed, perhaps in order to defend the collection to any
dissenters.

Paul attributes Titus' **earnest care** (*spoudē*) to God.
The Corinthians have already responded to Titus' visit
with **earnest care** (*spoudē*, 7:11), which has instilled in
Titus an **earnest care** for the Corinthians. But behind all
these events is God. It was God who comforted Paul with
the coming of Titus (7:4), and Titus was only the agent.
When Paul says **the same earnest care,** he probably means
the same earnest care that I have.

[17] Verse 6 says that Paul urged Titus to make this
visit. Titus, being **very earnest** (or "more earnest than
ever"), responded **of his own accord.** At verse 3, Paul
tells how the Macedonians gave "of their own free will."
The same Greek word, *authairetos,* describes Titus' response. Model Christian behavior is here, according to
Paul, voluntary; it does not require urging. Paul's reference

117

18 With him we are sending the brother who is famous among all the churches for his preaching of the gospel; 19 and not only that, but he has been appointed by the churches to travel with us in this gracious work which we are carrying on, for the glory of the Lord and to show our good will.

---

to Titus' good feelings toward the Corinthians should provide further motivation for them to give of their own accord. Very likely it is Titus who delivered this letter.

[18,19] Titus leads the delegation; two others accompany him (see vs. 22). The first is praised **in all the churches for his preaching.** What churches participated in this appointment is not known. The Macedonian churches are excluded, as is the Corinthian church. The Galatian churches participated in the collection (1 Cor. 16:1), and it is possible that they commissioned these men as envoys.

The anonymity of the two envoys who accompany Titus is particularly strange. One brother is **famous** (*epainos*, "praised by men"); the other is "tested" and "earnest" (vs. 22). If the Corinthians are to receive them, why does Paul not name them? Anonymity is often reserved for those who are dishonorable for some reason. Thus Paul does not mention the name of the immoral man in 1 Corinthians 5:1. The offender who had been so troublesome later at Corinth, mentioned in 2 Corinthians 2:5ff., is also left nameless. Some scholars hold the opinion (e.g., Lietzmann) that the name was originally there, but that the name was later erased because the brothers referred to lost their good reputation. That view does provide an explanation to a curious problem, but there is no manuscript evidence to support it.

Who were these traveling companions? Such names as Luke and Barnabas have been conjectured, but there is no evidence for that view. It is likely that the traveling companions mentioned in Acts 20:4 are intended here. These men were very likely representatives of the churches that have taken part in the collection. They are to accompany Paul to Jerusalem with the funds.

[20] We intend that no one should blame us about this liberal gift which we are administering, [21] for we aim at what is honorable not only in the Lord's sight but also in the sight of men. [22] And with them we are sending our brother whom we have often tested and found earnest in many matters, but who is now more earnest than ever because of his great confidence in you.

---

[20] Paul has placed a treasurer and trusted person in charge of the collection in order to avoid any implication of malfeasance of funds on his part. As 11:8, 9 shows, Paul was particularly sensitive to charges that he misused funds. At 2:17, Paul contrasts himself with certain peddlers of God's word. He may there have been answering the charge that he taught for money (see comments on 2:17). The gift was **liberal** or "abundant" (*hadrotēs*), and therefore special care was necessary. Paul often extols the virtue of being "blameless" (*amōmos*, Eph. 1:4; 5:27; Phil. 2:15). Consequently, Paul himself takes a precaution, lest he be **blamed** (*mōmēsētai*) or "censured," even when he is innocent.

[21] This verse is a reference to Proverbs 3:4 (see Rom. 12:17). Paul recognizes that not only the character, but also the apparent purpose of the Christian leader, is important. The Christian leader should not only be concerned that his conduct is pleasing to God; he also must be certain that his conduct appears **honorable** to men.

[22] Paul mentions here the second anonymous delegate (see vs. 18). Verse 23 indicates that he also has been chosen by the churches to be an envoy. By mentioning the **confidence** of the **brother** in the Corinthians, Paul hopes to provide further motivation for the Corinthians to give. He does not say whether the brother's confidence derived from Titus' report, or if the **brother** had known the Corinthians in the past. At verse 17, Paul said that Titus is "very earnest" (*spoudaioteros*). The same Greek word is used here of the **brother**, and is translated here **more earnest than ever**. Probably Titus' enthusiasm was contagious, causing the **brother** to share his earnestness.

²³ As for Titus, he is my partner and fellow worker in
your service; and as for our brethren, they are messengers *ʲ* of the churches, the glory of Christ. ²⁴ So give proof,
before the churches, of your love and of our boasting about
you to these men.
   ʲ Greek *apostles*

---

[23] With brief phrases Paul closes his "letter of
recommendation" for the three envoys. **Titus** is a **partner**
(*koinōnos*) and **fellow worker** (*sunergos*). His work is
described in 2 Corinthians 2:13; 7:4ff.; 12:18 and here. He
served, according to the letter written to him, as Paul's envoy on the island of Crete. The brothers are **messengers**
(*apostoloi*) **of the churches** and are, therefore, to be received with respect. Because of traveling false prophets in
Paul's day, it was important for Paul to assure the church
that these men were "commissioned." As the footnote to
the text shows, another word for **messengers** is "apostles."
The Greek word for "apostle" (*apostolos*) refers to anyone
who is sent as an envoy (see notes on 1:1). These **messengers** were apostles **of the churches** (see Phil. 2:25), not of
Christ (as were the Twelve and Paul). These men are
the glory of Christ. (One may compare here the expression at 1 Corinthians 11:7, where man is called the "glory
of God.") By reason of their integrity and Christian character, they bring glory to God's name.

[24] Once before, Paul had boasted to Titus of the
goodness of the Corinthian church, and they had not put
him to shame (7:14). The Corinthians must do more than
claim their love; they must **give proof before the churches.**
Their gift will be a public display of their **love** for Christ,
for Paul, and for the Judean churches. They will also be
displaying whether or not Paul's boasting is justified.

God's Blessings for the Generous Giver, 9:1-15

The repetition which is apparent in chapter 9 has led
many commentators to conclude that a fragment of another
letter has been inserted here. One gets the impression that

[1] Now it is superfluous for me to write to you about the offering for the saints,

---

8:24 is the conclusion of the discussion. Chapter 9 is indeed redundant, in that Paul begins anew what has already been covered. Furthermore, many have noted that chapter 9 proceeds as if it were approaching the subject without any prior notice, as if chapter 8 had not mentioned the collection. This curious redundancy can be explained, however, without resorting to the view that it is a later insertion. In the first place, the Greek word *gar* (for), which is not translated in the RSV, indicates that Paul is continuing a discussion already mentioned. In addition, Paul's great concern in chapter 9 leaves the impression that he felt much uncertainty about the Corinthian situation, and so much was at stake, that Paul decided to reinforce his position. False teachers at Corinth had been successful enough in undermining Paul's influence and in discouraging the Corinthians from participating in the collection, that Paul wishes to take no chances. Consequently, there is a reason for the repetition in chapter 9.

[1] At 8:4, 20, Paul referred to the collection as a "service" or "ministry" (*diakonia*), translated in those verses as "relief" (8:4) and by the verb "administering" (vs. 20). The same word is here translated **offering.** Jesus, who came as a servant, sanctified service for his disciples (see Luke 22:26ff.). His disciples are to learn that service is noble, and that disciples should serve each other. The giving of money represents one aspect of this service (cf. Acts 11:29; Rom. 15:30). The **offering** is, therefore, not an external necessity; it is a "service" or "ministry" in response to Christ, the servant. The **saints** are the poor of the Jerusalem churches.

The phrase, **it is superfluous** (*perisson*) **for me to write to you,** indicates that his added note is really more than is necessary for him. He wants added certainty, however, that he will not be embarrassed by them, after having boasted to others about them.

² for I know your readiness, of which I boast about you to the people of Macedonia, saying that Achaia has been ready since last year; and your zeal has stirred up most of them. ³ But I am sending the brethren so that our boasting about you may not prove vain in this case, so that you may be ready, as I said you would be;

---

[2] Paul's repeated boast has been that Achaia has been ready since last year. Last year is the same expression that is translated in 8:11 "a year ago" (*apo perusi*). Last year is preferable here, for he only means that a new year has begun since the project was initiated. Their readiness (*prothumia*) was mentioned at 8:12. It is interesting that Paul has boasted to the Macedonians about the Corinthians here, whereas at 8:1 he boasted to the Corinthians about the Macedonians (see notes on 8:1). Probably Paul's words here indicate a lag in the zeal of the Corinthians brought about by Paul's opponents. He reminds them of their enthusiasm last year in order to rekindle their great zeal.

Achaia was the Roman province of which Corinth was the chief city (see 1:1). Other congregations of Achaia were at Cenchrea (Rom. 16:1) and Athens (Acts 17:34).

The zeal (*zēlos*) of the Corinthians stirred up (*erethisen*) most of them (the Macedonians). Most of them (*tous pleiones*) does not indicate here that some of the Macedonians were unwilling to give. The word really means "the greatest number," and indicates that the Corinthian example had been so far-reaching that a "great number" had been stirred up. The word translated stirred up, (*erethizō*), is usually the word for quarreling, a connotation that does not fit here. Paul means here simply that the Macedonians had been inspired to a healthy rivalry by the Corinthian example.

[3] Here Paul tells why he is sending the brethren, mentioned at 8:18, 22. He does not mention the reason he gave at 8:20 ("that no one should blame" him of financial malfeasance). The reason given here was stated at 8:24: this is an opportunity to justify his boasting to them (see

[4] lest if some Macedonians come with me and find that you
are not ready, we be humiliated—to say nothing of you—
for being so confident. [5] So I thought it necessary to urge
the brethren to go on to you before me, and arrange in
advance for this gift you have promised, so that it may
be ready not as an exaction but as a willing gift.

7:4). Paul does not want to be "humiliated" (vs. 4) by
having his **boasting** prove **vain** (*kenoō*, "hollow" or
empty"). The **Brethren** are to precede him to be sure the
collection is ready.

[4] Just as their zeal had been a stimulus to the majority of Macedonians at one time, the waning of the Corinthians' zeal could have a depressing effect on the Macedonians who will be accompanying Paul. Furthermore,
Paul will soon be coming, and it would be embarrassing
indeed if the collection is unprepared when they see him.
Paul himself would be **humiliated.**

If leaves the question open whether or not there will
be Macedonians arriving with Paul. According to Acts
20:3, Paul "determined" to go through Macedonia on his
way to Corinth, and then to Jerusalem.

[5] Paul concludes here his reasons for sending the
brethren. Three times in this verse Paul uses in compound verbs the preposition "before" (*pro*). The brethren
are to **go before me** and **arrange in advance,** the (previously) **promised gift.** The emphasis here seems to be that
there has already been entirely too much delay and that
prompt completion of the task is urgent. The word for
the collection here is *eulogia,* translated as **gift** and as
willing gift. Paul's words for the collection in chapters 8—9
have consistently been devoid of any commercial connotation, probably because Paul is sensitive to charges
which his opponents could make. *Eulogia* is usually translated "blessing." In a few instances in the Old Testament
the word refers to a solemn gift (2 Kings 5:15). The
Christian is the recipient of God's grace. (Eph. 2:8) and
his blessing (Eph. 1:3). The Christian is not only the re-
ceiver of God's blessing; he responds to God's good-

⁶ The point is this: he who sows sparingly will also reap sparingly, and he who sows bountifully will also reap bountifully.

---

ness by being a source of "blessing" or offering to others.

In the last phrase of this verse, Paul contrasts the offering with an **exaction** (*pleonexia*). *Pleonexia* can also mean "greediness" or, as the KJV translates "covetousness." Paul does not want the gift to have the appearance of being grudgingly granted. The Corinthians might think that they are absolved from responsibility by giving the least possible sum. **A willing gift** or "blessing" is a response to one's blessings in Christ, and is by nature generous. The contrast in verse 6 indicates that the **willing gift** (*eulogia*) is by nature generous. There the same word is translated "bountifully."

[6] Verse 6 is the transition to the theme of this section (continuing through verse 15): that one should give **bountifully** to God. Apparently the Corinthians are under the impression that liberal giving will only cause them to suffer hardship later. Paul has responded to that kind of thinking already at 8:14.

The point is this is a phrase indicating that the words which follow are especially noteworthy (cf. 1 Cor. 7:29; 15:50, where the same expression is used). The quotation which follows is reminiscent of two Old Testament sayings. Proverbs 22:8 says, "He who sows injustice will reap calamity." According to Proverbs 11:24, "One man gives freely, yet grows all the richer; another withholds what he should give, and suffers only want." What Paul quotes has the sound of a popular maxim; perhaps it was in popular parlance in Paul's day. Paul takes a principle that has proved true in the moral realm and gives it a fiscal-moral meaning. His **point** is: do not withhold in sowing in order to have a good crop. The rewards of giving are in proportion to the degree of generosity. Paul does not say what it is that one **reaps bountifully**. The statement at 8:14 indicates that he is saying that on a human level those who are merciful obtain mercy from

⁷ Each one must do as he has made up his mind, not reluctantly or under compulsion, for God loves a cheerful giver. ⁸ And God is able to provide you with every blessing in abundance, so that you may always have enough of everything and may provide in abundance for every good work.

---

others in return. Verse 6 indicates that the giver will be replenished by God.

[7] Each will give according to how **he has made up his mind.** Paul's tactics with the church are not coercive. He does not "lord it over" their faith (1:24). When Paul encouraged Philemon to receive the runaway slave Onesimus, he stopped short of demanding compliance. He acted only with Philemon's "consent" (Phil. 14). The gift of the Macedonians was not coerced (8:3); it was "of their own free will." Money will not be extorted from the Corinthians in an emotional way; their giving will not be impulsive. It will be as **each has made up his mind.**

The word for **reluctantly** is literally "not from grief" (*mē ek lupēs*). The Corinthians have been moved to godly sorrow (*lupē*) by Paul's sorrowful letter. The purpose of the grief is not to stimulate their giving; it is to lead them to repentance. Paul here does not appeal to their recent grief as a motivation for giving. Nor is their giving to be **under compulsion** (*anagkēs*). The giver is not to be sad about giving, nor is the gift forced by Paul.

Paul's quotation is from Proverbs 22:8. There the Greek version which Paul read said, "God blesses a cheerful man and a giver." Paul makes **cheerful** modify **giver,** thus changing the emphasis. Just as God was not begrudging in showing his favor to man, man's response must be **cheerful.** Christian acts of goodness are not to be with "grumbling or questioning." Paul says at Romans 12:8, "He who does acts of mercy, with cheerfulness." Reception of the grace of God makes one cheerful, and drives out grumbling.

[8] Literally, Paul says, "God is able to make you excel in every grace." Paul has said at 8:7 that the Corin-

⁹ As it is written,
"He scatters abroad, he gives to the poor;
his righteousness ᵏ endures for ever."
ᵏ Or *benevolence*

---

thians "excel" (*perisseuein*) in everything; yet he hopes
they will excel in this "gracious work" or "grace" (*charis*).
As we have noticed previously, the collection is consistently described as a *charis*, or "grace" (see 8:1, 4, 19).
In reality, this giving is really God's grace through his
human agents. Verse 8 sounds here like the answer to
the objection which has apparently been voiced—that if
they are too generous now they might find themselves
in want later (see 8:14). Now Paul says that God, the
source of all grace (*charis* is rendered here **blessing**), will
always replenish those who participate in the grace of
giving. The result is that the Corinthians will always be
able to give. The **abundance** of God's gift is seen here in
the fact that Paul five times in verse 8 uses forms of *pas*,
translated "all" or "every." God will provide **every blessing**; they will **always** have "all sufficiency" in **everything**;
and they will be able to provide **for every good work.**

Since God's grace has no limits, there are no limits
to the Christian's act of giving. Since the Christian is the
agent of God's grace, the supply is not depleted. The
Christian always has **enough** (*autarkeia*), the word for
contentment; it does not carry the meaning in abundance.
Paul learned to have "contentment" (*autarkeia*), despite
privation (Phil. 4:11-13), because of "Christ who
strengthens" him. Paul does not suggest that Christianity
is a sound business investment bringing material reward
for liberal giving.

God replenishes, says Paul, that you **may provide in
abundance for every good work,** and not for any selfish
use. **Enough** is not only sufficiency for oneself but also
for one's brothers. The "contentment" (*autarkeia,* **enough**)
comes only when others have a share in it.

[9] Paul enforces his words with a quotation from
Psalm 112:9, which speaks of the righteous man. **He scat-**

¹⁰ He who supplies seed to the sower and bread for food will supply and multiply your resources ¹ and increase the harvest of your righteousness.ᵏ ¹¹ You will be enriched in every way for great generosity, which through us will produce thanksgiving to God.

ⁱ Greek *sowing*
ᵏ Or *benevolence*

---

ters, gives liberally and wherever needed; the opposite is "sowing sparingly" (vs. 6). **He gives to the poor,** as the Corinthians are being asked to do. **Righteousness** (*dikaiosunē*) is not used here in the common Pauline sense. The common Pauline meaning is that of the right relationship with God which is conferred by God through Christ (see Rom. 3:21-25). Here the word is used in the same sense that one finds in Matthew 6:1, where Jesus warns against doing one's **righteousness** before men. There **righteousness** is a technical term for almsgiving. Here **righteousness** and **every good work** (vs. 8) are synonymous. They are expressed in the giving of money.

[10] The farmer does not depend on his own resources but on God. The quotation is from Isaiah 55:10, where the prophet praises the Lord, who gives "seed for the sower and bread to the eater." The prophet's statement suggests the absolute assurance of his faith in the promises of God. In the same way, the Corinthians can be certain of God's faithfulness to provide. At 1 Corinthians 3:6, 7, Paul says that God is the one who gives the growth to the harvest. By using these agricultural figures, Paul emphasizes the point of verse 8: the Corinthians need not fear a depletion of their **resources.** God provides and will multiply their ability to give. Moffatt's translation is apt: "He will increase the crop of your charities." The closing words are from Hosea 10:12. The Corinthians' responsibility at the moment is to plant. Just as God multiplies the seed in proportion to the amount planted in the physical world, the Corinthians can give liberally, having assurance that their "planting" will be increased.

[11] Verse 11 is a summary statement of what has

gone before. **In every way** (or "in everything") recalls
the thought of verse 8. The giver is blessed by God in
order to enrich others, and the blessing is unlimited. The
thought of verse 8 is clear here also, that the blessings for
liberality can never be used for selfish reasons. One who
gives is **enriched** (*ploutizomenoi*); but what he receives
is not a return on an investment that can be used for
selfish reasons. The enrichment which God gives is sufficient **for great generosity** (*haplotēs*, translated "liberality"
at 8:2). The word signifies "singleness of purpose." The
same word is used at 11:3 to mean "sincere dedication."
According to Colossians 3:22, slaves are to obey with
"singleness of heart" (*haplotēs*). The word signifies one
whose motives are unmixed, who has only one aim. When
the word is applied to the giving of money, it is natural
that one who is singlemindedly devoted to Christ would
be compelled to be generous. Paul has given the Corinthians the example of the Macedonians with regard to
their liberality (8:2); he hopes now that the example of
the Macedonians will be the motivation for the Corinthians to practice generosity.

Paul adds a point here which will be taken up in the
next few verses. This gift taken to Jerusalem through
Paul's agency **(through us) will produce thanksgiving**
(*eucharistian*) to God's glory. By indicating his part in
the collection, and by showing that his part leads to
God's glory, Paul is probably anticipating any charges
that he was not to be trusted with a generous gift. Paul
answers that his part leads to God's glory. **Thanksgiving**
is the natural response to the grace of God, since grace
is a gift. In 4:15, Paul says that the grace of God leads to
thanksgiving on the part of man. This grace was made
known by Jesus Christ, who "for your sake became poor"
(8:9); now all of life is a **thanksgiving** to him (9:15). To
take part in this collection is no trivial matter; it means
nothing less than participation in God's grace (8:1). Consequently, those who receive this grace will naturally be
led to **thanksgiving.**

¹² **for the rendering of this service not only supplies the wants of the saints but also overflows in many thanksgivings to God.**

---

[12] In 8:14, Paul said that equality was the ideal; the Corinthians should not let their brothers be in want. One reason for participating in the collection is to supply their **wants** (see 8:14). The collection on this level is a compassionate gesture to relieve the Jerusalem poor from hunger. On another level, it **overflows in many thanksgivings to God.** If the Corinthians "overflow" in "every good work" (vs. 8), the natural result will be that the poor of Jerusalem will overflow in thanksgiving. Paul's purpose in his work was that "many will give thanks" (1:11). They will respond to God's grace, and Paul's labor will be worthwhile. The **thanksgiving** which Paul describes here has the result of bringing the Jewish and Gentile Christians closer together. The giving of their means on the part of the Corinthians will cause such **thanksgiving** that the old cultural barriers will be removed (see Rom. 15:27). The collection was more than a humanitarian gesture; it was a means of establishing closer fellowship.

The RSV translates here, **the rendering of this service** (*hē diakonia tēs leitourgias,* literally, "the ministry of this service"). Paul in chapters 8—9 has consistently referred to the collection as a "ministry" or "service" (*diakonia,* 8:4; 9:1, 12, 13; cf. Acts 11:29). The word translated **service** here (*leitourgia*) is common in the Old Testament and in the Greek world. It is the word from which "liturgy" is derived. The verb form of this word is used when Paul discusses the collection in Romans 15:27 and is translated "be of service." In the Old Testament, the word signifies the ceremonial service of a priest. Since in the New Testament Jesus is the true high priest, the word is applied to his **service** before God for man (Heb. 8:2ff.). The church is a "royal priesthood" (1 Peter 2:5); it has no special priesthood which offers a **service** on behalf of others. Since every Christian is a priest, the church

¹³ Under the test of this service, you ᵐ will glorify God
by your obedience in acknowledging the gospel of Christ,
and by the generosity of your contribution for them and
for all others;

ᵐ Or *they*

---

together responds in **service** or *leitourgeia*. Paul thus
speaks of the collection in terms far removed from commercial terminology. For these Corinthians who were unconcerned or even adamant against the collection, Paul
says that the collection is no less than the service of the
"royal priesthood" (1 Peter 2:5), the church.

[13] The collection will be a **test** of the quality of the
Corinthians' **service**. *Diakonia*, **service,** is a necessary
Christian response to Christ himself, who came as a "servant" (Luke 22:24-27). The Macedonians have already
survived the **test** (8:2) by giving in the midst of affliction.
The Corinthians have not thought of **service** as a **test**
(*dokimē*) of their commitment to Christ. They have, because of Paul's unimpressive appearance, wanted some
"proof" (or **test**, *dokimē*) that Christ is speaking through
Paul (13:3). The **test** for the Corinthians, or at least for
Paul's opponents, has been one's outward appearance
(10:18). Those who "commended themselves" by eloquence (11:5, 6) or by spiritual gifts (12:1-8) thought
these were the tests of their service to God, and thus they
called themselves "servants of righteousness" (11:15).
The true servant, according to Paul, is one who imitates
his Lord, who follows him in weakness (12:9, 10) and
self-sacrifice. Thus the **test** of their **service** is whether or
not the Corinthians follow Jesus in their willingness to
give.

This **test** will cause God to be glorified. In Greek,
glorify is a participle (*doxazontes*), and it is unclear who
will glorify God. It could be either the Jerusalem poor
or the Corinthians. The RSV rendering **you will glorify
God** is probably correct, since it is the Corinthians who
will be surviving the **test**. God will be glorified in two
ways. Their **obedience in acknowledging the gospel** will

¹⁴ while they long for you and pray for you, because of the surpassing grace of God in you. ¹⁵ Thanks be to God for his inexpressible gift!

---

be proved. The Corinthians have acknowledged or made a "confession" (*homologia*) of their acceptance of Christ. Perhaps Paul is referring to their pre-baptismal confession, in which they originally made confession (*homologia;* cf. Heb. 3:1; 4:14). But such a confession or acknowledgment is meaningful only when **obedience** is involved, in this case in regard to the collection. God will be glorified when their **generosity** or "singleness of purpose" (*haplotēs*) strengthened the fellowship (*koinōnia*) between Jewish and Gentile churches. Their **contribution** (*koinōnia*, "fellowship") was a means of sharing with the Jerusalem Christians; it was a test of how devoted they are to enhancing this fellowship.

[14] Verse 14 expresses the hope of a tightening of the bonds of affection between the Jewish and Gentile churches. As Paul was the apostle to the Gentiles, but was himself trained in Jerusalem, there was for him the great dream of bringing together Jewish and Gentile Christianity. He had played a significant role whenever there was a strain which their diverse backgrounds caused (cf. Gal. 2:1-10; Acts 15). In a day when Christianity was threatened with division into two groups, Paul made every effort to bring them together into one brotherhood. The contribution, although it has not yet been completed, has already had its effect: it has caused the Jerusalemites to **long for** and **pray for** the Corinthians. What the Corinthians are participating in is no commercial venture; it is **the grace of God** (see 3:2).

[15] The thought of the Jewish and Gentile churches bound so closely together leads Paul to this concluding doxology. God's grace is **inexpressible** or "inexhaustible." His gift is Jesus Christ (8:9). The gift includes God's constant providing for those who share in the act of giving (9:8), and it includes the experience of fellowship.

131

All Christian activity is a thanksgiving for God's **inexpressible gift.** Paul appeals to the Corinthians' experience of gratitude to motivate them to give.

PAUL'S VINDICATION AGAINST HIS OPPONENTS, 10:1—13:10

Defense Against False Leaders, 10:1—11:15

At chapter 10, Paul begins the last major section of 2 Corinthians. One needs to read only the first few verses of chapter 10 to become aware of the complete change of tone. No more mention is made of Paul's confidence or joy in the Corinthians, or the boasting that he has done on their behalf (cf. 7:4; 9:2). At chapters 10—13, the tone of Paul's message is stern. The entire section (10—13) is "a lively self-defense of the apostle against the charges of his opponents, together with stern warnings for the church" (Lietzmann, p. 139). In chapters 10—13, Paul is "no longer the father reconciled with his children, giving them advice full of benevolence, but an irritated chief, who is defending himself by attacking his opponents" (Hering, p. 69).

The change of tone which marks chapters 10—13 is indeed striking. Would Paul end an epistle marked with such joy (see 7:4) on this agitated note? A great number of biblical scholars find this abrupt change of tone at chapters 10—13 so different from chapters 1—9 that the conclusion is widespread that chapters 10—13 were originally a part of separate letter. Since Paul himself mentions a letter written "out of much affliction and anguish" (2:4), it is conceivable that chapters 10—13 were written before 1—9, and that they are a part of that "sorrowful" letter (see Introduction).

The view that chapters 10—13 are at least part of that sorrowful letter is not to be dismissed lightly. Yet it must be seen that chapters 10—13 are not really as out of place here as some suggest. It is plausible that chapters 1—9 represent Paul's statement to the church, whereas chapters

¹ I, Paul, myself entreat you, by the meekness and
gentleness of Christ—I who am humble when face to
face with you, but bold to you when I am away!—

10—13 give his defense to his opponents. His statement
to the church is filled with joy and confidence in them;
his defense before his opponents reflects the bitter strug-
gle they had caused.

It seems apparent also that there are too many connecting links between 1—9 and 10—13 to think that they
were not written at the same time. Both sections are concerned with those who "commend themselves" (3:1; 5:12;
10:12); Titus' trip to them is still in the planning stage
in 1—9 and 10—13 (12:18; 8:16-21); and there is deep
concern over one's right to boast (5:12; cf. 11:18).

The change of Paul's temperament from joy to bitterness is not really strange. Paul frequently appends a warning directed at his opponents at the close of his letters.
Thus Paul at 1 Corinthians 16:22, in the midst of final
greetings, says, "If anyone has no love for the Lord, let
him be accursed." In Romans 16:17, in the context of
final greetings, Paul gives a final warning for the church
to "take note of those who create dissensions and difficulties." This same kind of warning is found at Galatians
6:11-17. Thus the stern nature of chapters 10—13 is in-
tegral to Paul's message to the church there and is not
to be separated from 1—9, although the change of tone
is striking.

[1] Paul begins his defense with a note of authority,
I, Paul, myself is an authoritative, emphatic way of saying "I." It means "I and no one else." What is to follow
is weighty; Paul's authority is under attack. The expression calls special attention to his unique authority in order
to give support to the warning which follows. Paul does
not refer to himself by name often (cf. 1 Cor. 16:21; Gal.
5:2; Col. 1:23; 4:18; 1 Thess. 2:18; 2 Thess. 3:17; Phile.
9, 19). When he does, his purpose is to emphasize his
apostolic authority. Sometimes the **I, Paul** indicates the
point at which Paul takes his pen from his amanuensis

to add his signature (cf. 1 Cor. 16:21; Col. 4:18; Gal. 6:11). That is not likely the case here. The closest parallel to Paul's emphatic **I, Paul** is Galatians 5:2; there, however, Paul does not appear to write until 6:11, where he says, "See what large letters I write with my own hand."

Paul does not command, even though he speaks with authority. Rather, he chooses to **entreat** or "exhort" (*parakalein*). Paul's epistles abound in exhortations of this nature (cf. Rom. 12:1; 1 Thess. 4:1; Phil. 4:2; Eph. 4:1). Paul never entreats his readers on the basis of personal loyalty; they are encouraged on the basis of what God has done in Christ. Their motivation for action is Christ. Thus Paul exhorts "by the mercies of God" (Rom. 12:1); "in the Lord Jesus" (1 Thess. 4:1); and "by our Lord Jesus and the love of the Spirit" (Rom. 15:30). Here his exhortation is **by the meekness and gentleness of Christ**. There is a special reason why Paul speaks here of **meekness** and **gentleness** as two characteristics of Jesus. He is saying that those are traits of Jesus which must be imitated by the Christian community; therefore, Paul himself has imitated the **meekness and gentleness** of Christ. But in imitating Jesus in this manner, Paul's opponents have pointed to Paul's **meekness** as a sign of weakness (cf. 11:29, 30), and therefore a sign that he was inferior to certain "superlative apostles" (12:11).

Paul appealed to his sufferings as the sign that he was the true apostle. His defense does not spring from his position, but from his sufferings (6:4ff.). By "carrying about in his body the death of Jesus" (4:10), he is only imitating his Lord. His "weakness" is only an opportunity for the power of God (12:10). Thus **meekness and gentleness** are not signs of weakness; they are indications that it is Paul, and not his opponents, who is the true apostle. Therefore, Paul's authority is not to be questioned.

Meekness was not considered a virtue among Paul's opponents, who were concerned with position (10:13-18). Nevertheless, an important Christian virtue is **meekness** (*praus, prautētos*). Paul may have in mind a saying similar to Matthew 11:29, in which Jesus says, "I am meek

²I beg of you that when I am present I may not have to show boldness with such confidence as I count on showing against some who suspect us of acting in worldly fashion.

(*praus*). . . ." One of the beatitudes pronounces a blessing upon the meek (Matt. 5:5). The word does not suggest cowardice or a spineless acceptance of bad circumstances; the word suggests strength under control. **Gentleness** (*epieikeia*) is likewise not a word for passivity. It suggests one who, although he is provoked, is able to maintain a generous attitude (see Phil. 4:5, where the word is translated "forbearance").

The opponents have charged that Paul is **humble** (*tapeinos*) in their presence. A better word for **humble** would be "obsequious" or "groveling." **Humble** may suggest a favorable connotation to our ears, where none is intended here. The charge is repeated in verse 10, where Paul's critics say that his bodily presence is "weak." In eloquence and other qualities necessary for a missionary he left much to be desired (11:5f.; 12:11). The charge is not without foundation, for at 1 Corinthians 2:3, Paul says, "I was with you in weakness and in much fear and trembling." But what the opponents see as a disqualification for apostleship, Paul sees as a prerequisite. Only in his weakness can he give opportunity for the working of God's power and imitate his Lord (6:3ff.; 12:10).

[2] Paul mentions at 9:5 his plans to visit the Corinthians. Here Paul requests of the Corinthians that circumstances be so favorable that he would not need to show his capacity for **boldness.** Nevertheless, there are **some** against whom Paul intends to act. Not only have they accused Paul of being humble or "obsequious" (vs. 1); they accuse him of acting **in worldly fashion** (literally, "walking according to the flesh"). The fact that Paul is humble (vs. 1) or "weak" (vs. 10), and that he does not have the gift of speech (10:10; 11:6) is proof for Paul's opponents that he does not have the Spirit. The opponents point to Paul's change of travel plans for evi-

³ **For though we live in the world we are not carrying on a worldly war,**

dence that he is a weak, vacillating creature, who acts **in worldly fashion** and not according to the Spirit (1:17). Paul's **worldly** ways are seen also in the accusation that he is "crafty" (12:16; cf. 4:2) in his methods. What Paul shows as the unmistakable sign that he is a true apostle and that he is true to his Lord (his weakness), his opponents see as a sign that he does not have the Spirit, and is, therefore, not a true apostle.

[3] Paul makes an important distinction which his opponents do not make. For them, to be in the Spirit is to be delivered from all fleshly concerns. Paul, however, distinguishes between being "in the flesh" (*en sarki*) and living "according to the flesh." The RSV renders this contrast as one of being **in the world** and being **worldly**. Although the Christian is a new creature (5:17) and lives in the realm of the Spirit, he remains **in the world** (literally, "in the flesh"). To live in this way is to be exposed to all of the limitations which bodily existence contains, including suffering and death. This is the realm of faith, and not of sight (5:7; Gal. 2:20).

We do not carry on a worldly war ("we do not war according to the flesh"). To live "according to the flesh" is to live in sin. Christians walk "not after the flesh, but after the Spirit" (Rom. 8:4-7). The state of opposition to God and Christ can be described simply as to live "according to the flesh" (Rom. 8:5), for those who live in this way "mind the things of the flesh": their whole outlook is determined by **worldly** considerations. The Christian, as a "new creature" (5:17), has the gift of the Spirit, and for him the "old has passed away." He no longer judges from a "human point of view" ("according to the flesh," 5:16), for his life is determined by the Spirit (5:5; cf. Rom. 8:5, 9).

Paul uses once again the metaphor of **war** to describe the Christian life. At 6:7, he has already mentioned the weapons of this warfare, as he does again at 10:4. As so

⁴ **for the weapons of our warfare are not worldly but have divine power to destroy strongholds.**

frequently in the New Testament, life is thought to be the battlefield where God and Satan wage war (see Eph. 6:10ff.). Paul is God's soldier in this **war** (1 Cor. 9:7). His opponents accuse him of conducting himself as the unredeemed man, one who walks according to the flesh. Paul responds: this is not a **worldly** ("fleshly") **war**. Paul lives by God's Spirit.

[4] This comparison of his labors to a military campaign is one of Paul's favorite themes (cf. Phil. 1:30; 2 Tim. 4:7; Eph. 6:11ff.). Paul's opponents have mistaken Paul's methods (meekness, gentleness, vs. 1) for weakness (vs. 10). Christ, his ministry, his cross, seem weak to the worldly man (1 Cor. 1:18-25). But God chose "what is weak in the world" to shame the strong (1 Cor. 1:27). This weakness was evident in the cross of Christ (13:4), which to the worldly man was the epitome of human weakness. Paul's opponents confuse **power** with position (10:12-18) and eloquence (11:6). Since Paul carries around "the death of Jesus" in his body (4:10), he must therefore be using worldly weapons, says his opponents.

Paul's opponents were being worldly in their appraisal. What they confuse for weakness has **divine power** to achieve its purpose. Paul is able, by this divine power, **to destroy strongholds.** The word here for **destroy** (*kathairein*) is used here and at 10:8; 13:10 to signify the work to which God has called Paul. God has given him powers either to destroy or build. His mission is similar in scope to Jeremiah's, "to destroy . . . and to build" (Jer. 1:10; cf. 1 Cor. 3:10-15). As 13:10 indicates, Paul's purpose was to build up. He will **destroy** only when this task is forced upon him. **Strongholds** (*ochurōma*) are "fortified places" of the enemy. Paul's weapons may have the appearance of weakness, but they are suitable for the kind of war he is engaged in. Worldly men did not understand that the cross represented God's power (1 Cor. 1:18). Nor do Paul's worldly opponents realize that God's power is avail-

137

⁵ **We destroy arguments and every proud obstacle to the knowledge of God, and take every thought captive to obey Christ,**

---

able only in human weakness (13:4). Paul knows that when he is "weak," then he is "strong" with God's power (12:10).

[5] What is this enemy stronghold which Paul is able to destroy? At verse 5, Paul names **arguments** (*logismoi*, literally, "reasonings"). These **arguments** amount to an overestimation of man's rational intelligence, and therefore they shut a man off from God by causing excessive pride. Such **arguments** cannot be destroyed by worldly weapons. The Corinthians had been from the first impressed by human wisdom (1 Cor. 2:5). It is to be remembered that Paul's opponents have exploited their gift of eloquence (11:6) which was for them a sign of the Spirit's presence. But their gifts led only to human pride (10:12, 13) and boasting. Their weapons turned out to be worldly. Paul's weapon to **destroy arguments** is the power of God which he has experienced by accepting for himself the cross of Christ and the weakness that such a life involves.

Paul destroys also **every proud obstacle to the knowledge of God.** The **proud obstacle** is another military figure for a high, well-guarded military fortress. This **obstacle** is human pride or human wisdom. One cannot **destroy** this **obstacle** with worldly weapons such as human intelligence or outward position. The world can never know God through wisdom (1 Cor. 1:21). The cross of Christ is man's only way of knowing God. The cross is the only weapon which has the power to **destroy** human pride. For this reason, Paul had taken as his weapon the cross of Christ, for in it is **the knowledge of God** and the destruction of human pride.

Paul's military language continues. He intends to **take every thought captive to obey Christ.** The image is that of military campaigns in which the victor took prisoners captive with him. Paul does not use force because he

⁶ being ready to punish every disobedience, when your obedience is complete.

⁷ Look at what is before your eyes. If any one is confident that he is Christ's, let him remind himself that as he is Christ's, so are we.

---

wants to do more than win arguments. He wants to take every thought (*noēma*) captive. The use of force might have made a more impressive victory for the moment; but by employing weakness, Paul is able to capture every thought, i.e., he is able not only to force submission but to win loyalty. *Noēma*, translated thought, is used five times in 2 Corinthians, and usually the word signifies man's unredeemed state of mind (at 2:11 it is translated "designs"; at 3:14 it is used of "hardened minds"; at 4:4 it is used of "blinded minds"; and at 11:3, Paul is concerned, lest their minds be "led astray"). No human efforts, no rational arguments, are adequate to captivate a man's will. The cross of Christ, because it exhibits God's love and is able to break down human pride, is the only weapon which can win man's loyalty. For that reason Paul comes in the weakness which characterized Christ.

[6] Paul has already said that the test of the Corinthians' obedience is in their willingness to participate in the collection (9:13). Closely involved with that test is their willingness to punish the agitators. Paul previously mentioned that the Corinthians have already punished the offender who led in opposition to him (2:9; 7:15). Such punishment was probably exclusion from the fellowship of the church. Paul is still concerned that the Corinthians will not discipline the other offenders; until they do, their obedience is not complete. Paul is concerned (vs. 5) that they obey Christ in order that they may really belong to him (vs. 7). Yet, as long as there is any rebellion there, their obedience is incomplete, and they do not belong to Christ. He plans to come again to Corinth (13:2), and when he does he "will not spare them."

[7] In verses 1-6, Paul has spoken as an authoritative

139

Christian leader. He now warns his readers not to let any
other person's claim to authority obscure his own authority. The RSV renders the opening statement, **Look at what
is before your eyes,** as an imperative, meaning, "Look at
this obvious fact." But the verb for **look** (*blepete*) can
also be an indicative. If so, Paul is saying, "You judge by
outward appearance" (literally, "according to the face").
The latter interpretation seems to be more probable since
Paul elsewhere accuses his opponents of judging by a
worldly standard (cf. vss. 1-6; 12-18). The use of the
wrong standard has confused his readers as to who really
is **Christ's.** The word **Christ's** (literally, "of Christ") is the
normal way of saying in Greek what is expressed by the
word "Christian," namely, one who belongs or adheres to
Christ.

Both Paul and his opponents claim to be "servants of
Christ" (11:23) and "apostles" (11:5). The confusing
thing for the Corinthians is that Paul and the opponents
use two different criteria to make their claim. The opponents base their claim on outward manifestations: visions (12:1ff.) and mighty works (12:12). They claim that
Paul is worldly (vs. 2), and therefore he is not **Christ's.**
Since he does not have the gift of eloquence, they wish
to see some proof that Christ is speaking through Paul
(13:3). Paul bases his claim on the fact of his sufferings
(11:23ff.; 12:10; 6:4ff.). He is **Christ's** because he participates in the suffering of Christ.

It has been conjectured that those who claim to be
Christ's are the "Christ party" of 1 Corinthians 1:12. This
view is hardly tenable since the special problems of
1 Corinthians 1 are not in evidence here. Furthermore, it
is not certain that a distinct "Christ party" is referred to
at 1 Corinthians 1:12. The opponents here are claiming in
a special way to be "servants of Christ" (11:23). They
may be claiming a special relationship to Christ through
personal acquaintance with the Jesus of the flesh. They
appear to claim that, although they are "servants of
Christ," Paul is not. Paul makes no claim to superiority
over his opponents (see 11:5). Paul simply claims that he

⁸ For even if I boast a little too much of our authority, which the Lord gave for building you up and not for destroying you, I shall not be put to shame. ⁹ I would not seem to be frightening you with letters.

---

has as much commission from Christ (see 4:1) as they do.

[8] **Boast** is a key word in chapters 10—13. The word is used in chapters 1—9 of Paul's glad confidence in his readers (7:4, 14; 8:24); in chapters 10—13 the word is used in a defensive tone. Paul is extremely cautious about boasting, even though he feels compelled to (11:16; 12:6). One feels that Paul is embarrassed about needing to **boast**. To be Christ's means for Paul to have **authority** (*exousia*) from him. Mention of this **authority** from the Lord here and at 13:10 indicates that a lively issue centers around Paul's use of authority. Paul's opponents point to his humility as a sign that he could not have apostolic authority. Because Paul's **authority** as an apostle is questioned, he is careful to point out that his ministry is from God (4:1; 5:19, 20), and not his own undertaking.

The apostlic authority is for **building up** and not for **destroying** the church, although Paul is capable of doing both. It is probable here that Paul is alluding to Jeremiah 1:10 (see vs. 4). Paul's mission is clearly to **build** on the foundation, which is Christ (see 1 Cor. 3:10-15). The reference to destruction is no doubt directed at Paul's opponents who have had harmful influence on the church. No one invested with true apostolic authority would destroy the church, as they have. Paul's actions have indicated, however, that his one purpose was their "upbuilding" (12:19) or edification. Christian behavior, and especially apostolic behavior, would aim for that which builds up the church. Because of Paul's actions, he has no reason to **be put to shame** or "disgraced"; he has used his **authority** in a responsible way. He has made no threat which he cannot carry out, and his behavior will confirm what he has said by letter.

[9] Paul does not wish to be one whose purpose is nothing more than to elicit fear (see Gal. 4:20). He can

¹⁰ For they say, "His letters are weighty and strong, but his bodily presence is weak, and his speech of no account." ¹¹ Let such people understand that what we say by letter when absent, we do when present. ¹² Not that we venture to class or compare ourselves with some of those who commend themselves. But when they measure themselves by one another, and compare themselves with one another, they are without understanding.

---

make good what he says. He has been accused of writing more forcefully than he acts.

[10] Paul's authority was at stake. His weakness was a sign that he could not wield apostolic authority. For that reason he was stern only in his **letters,** never when he was face to face. His letters are **weighty** (literally, "hard to bear") and **strong** (*ischuros*). The word for **weighty** (*bareiai*) can also mean "severe in the use of apostolic authority." It is opposite in meaning from the weakness (*asthenēs*) of Paul's appearance. The word **strong** (*ischuros*) is opposite in meaning to **of no account** (*exouthenēmenos*). Thus Paul created a completely different impression through his letters from that which was created through his personal appearance, causing him to appear "two-faced." In person, he is **weak** (*asthenēs*) and "humble" (vs. 1), certainly not authoritative. This weakness is explained further here by his lack of eloquence (see 11:6). Paul himself said that his first preaching was not in "plausible words of wisdom" (1 Cor. 2:4). This lack of the gift of speech means for Paul's opponents that Paul is a worldly man (vs. 2) who does not have the gift of the Spirit. But Paul accepts the charge that he is **weak,** for that is a sign of apostleship. Christ himself was "crucified in weakness, but lives by the power of God" (13:4).

[11] For those who question his authority (vs. 8) by saying that he is incapable of showing authority, Paul responds here. If he comes and finds that they have not accepted his authority, they will learn that he can be stern in person (cf. 12:20; 13:2, 10).

[12] Verses 12-18 are concerned with the subject of

¹³ But we will not boast beyond limit, but will keep to
the limits God has apportioned us, to reach even to you.

boasting. Paul's opponents have tried to undermine his
authority by comparing his weakness (vss. 1-11) with
their impressive appearance (see Rom. 12:3). Paul's boasting (vs. 8) is nothing compared to the boasting of his
opponents. Paul remarks, a little caustically, that he does
not wish to get involved in the business of comparing, as
some do. That the opponents commend themselves has
been noticed at 3:1; 5:12. They flaunt their gifts of the
Spirit, and they measure themselves by one another. They
measure by human, self-established standards. They constantly compare themselves (*sugkrinontes*) with each
other; only those who judge by worldly standards would
become involved in comparing. This fact is proof that they
are without spiritual understanding. The judgments they
have made on Paul (vss. 1, 10) show that they, not Paul,
are worldly in their standards (see vs. 2).

[13] Those who have no standard but themselves resort to boasting beyond limit (*ametron*). This boasting
beyond limit seems to be identified in verse 15 as a boasting in "other men's labors." The boasting of Paul's opponents is beyond limit because they have come into his
sphere of activity and made Paul's own work the subject
of their boasting. Paul, however, will keep to the limits
God has apportioned us (literally, "according to the
measure of the canon God has apportioned us"). *Kanōn*,
translated limits, was originally a measuring rod. For Paul,
it is the norm for judging between right and wrong. Paul
says here that God has placed a norm, and that he will
live by it. Twice more the word *kanōn* is used in this context, and in verses 15 and 16, the word is translated "field."
The KJV consistently translates the word as "rule." What
is this "rule" or limit (*kanōn*) which God has given? The
RSV has interpreted the word geographically, as a field or
"sphere of activity." That view is basically correct. Paul
was the first to preach Christ in Corinth. God, therefore,
allotted Corinth as his field or sphere of activity. When

¹⁴ **For we are not overextending ourselves, as though we did not reach you; we were the first to come all the way to you with the gospel of Christ.** ¹⁵ **We do not boast beyond limit in other men's labors; but our hope is that as your faith increases, our field among you may be greatly enlarged,**

---

outsiders came to Corinth, they came into Paul's sphere of labor. But God had given Paul the right to establish and develop the church at Corinth (Acts 18:9f.).

Elsewhere in his epistle Paul took seriously the fact that there was a field or "norm" for him which was to be understood geographically. Thus in Galatians 2:8-10, Paul agrees with Jewish Christians that his field of work will be among Gentiles, and in Romans, which Paul writes from Corinth at the end of his labors in this area, Paul alludes to his geographic program for his missionary work (see Rom. 15:23-28). Only after he has exhausted his territory is he free to go to Rome and beyond.

[14] The reference here is to Paul's opponents. Paul had broken new ground. The intruders had gone where they had not been sent by God. Paul had accepted God's standard (*kanōn*, "field," vs. 15). His work in Corinth was under the guidance of the Spirit of God. At Corinth Paul was not **overextending** himself. It was in the area which God had designated for him.

[15] To boast of one's own labor is perfectly normal, as long as one boasts in the Lord. Thus Paul has not refrained from boasting (Rom. 15:17f.; 1 Cor. 15:10), for the Corinthians are Paul's grounds for boasting (2 Cor. 1:14). He has boasted of the Corinthians' willingness to give (9:3) and of his visions and revelations (12:1). But his boasting is not **beyond limit**. He never compares his work with that of others; he never boasts in the **labors** of someone else. God has given Paul his own sphere of activity, his own **limit**, and in that only does he **boast**. When his opponents boast **in other men's labors** (Paul's), they only prove that they do not adhere to the **limits** which God has given.

144

¹⁶ so that we may preach the gospel in lands beyond you, without boasting of work already done in another's field. ¹⁷ "Let him who boasts, boast of the Lord." ¹⁸ For it is not the man who commends himself that is accepted, but the man whom the Lord commends.

In the second part of the verse, Paul hints at his future plans. His plans depend on an increase of **faith** among the Corinthians. Before Paul can do anything else, the problems at Corinth must be satisfactorily settled. The present crisis has the effect of tying Paul to Corinth. Before he can go somewhere else, his work at Corinth (**our field**) must be **enlarged** (*megalunthēnai*).

[16] Verse 16 gives expression to Paul's dream of preaching **in lands beyond** the territory covered by his missionary journeys. His ambition is "to preach the gospel, not where Christ has already been named" (Rom. 15:20), lest he build on another's foundation. This program of evangelism included Rome (Acts 19:21) and even Spain (Rom. 15:28). He wants to do the kind of pioneering work there that he has done in Corinth. He does not want to boast of work done in another's field or "build on another's foundation" (Rom. 15:20). At Corinth, Paul had "planted" (1 Cor. 3:6) and "laid the foundation" (1 Cor. 3:10). Paul uses here a third time the word *kanōn*, translated **field** (see vs. 15; "limits," vs. 13). God's norm or standard is for Paul to do pioneering work.

[17] In words already quoted in 1 Corinthians 1:31, Paul paraphrases Jeremiah 9:23, 24. Paul issues here a fundamental criticism of his opponents. They take credit for work Paul has done in Corinth. No Christian should **boast** or take credit for his work, unless he boasts of what Christ does through him. There was always for Paul the consciousness that there were no grounds for boasting, apart from Jesus Christ. **Let him boast . . . of the Lord,** who has given him strength to achieve his mission and a **field** of labor in which to work.

[18] Verse 18 summarizes the fundamental idea of

¹ I wish you would bear with me in a little foolishness. Do bear with me!

---

verses 12-17, and of much of the entire book. Paul has referred a number of times to his opponents' custom of "commending themselves" (3:1, 4:2; 5:12; 10:12). But in all of this, they are not commended by God. They have interferred in Paul's missionary activity, a place in which Paul has been commended by God. No one who interferes in this manner can be **accepted** (*dokimos*) by God or by the church. The word *dokimos* also means a "test." The opponents have used arbitrary tests to declare Paul unfit for his work (10:1, 10), having decided that Paul is "worldly" (10:2), and not spiritual. Paul says, however, that they have failed the test which God gives by not following his guidance on the mission field (vs. 15).

[1] In chapter 11, Paul continues his self-defense of his apostleship against those who belittle his work and contest the validity of his apostleship. This chapter is very important for its description of what true apostleship involves (11:23ff.). It is also important in providing some details about Paul's life which are unpublished elsewhere. Paul's epistles seldom provide any biographical data either about his outward state or his inward concerns. Acts is useful in supplying details about Paul's outward circumstances, even though the information there leaves many gaps. Only 2 Corinthians and Galatians, two epistles in which Paul defended himself vigorously, provide considerable autobiographical information.

The defense in chapter 11 arises from Paul's concern that the Corinthians may yet be enticed by the false apostles. The two words that are keys to the discussion are "foolishness" or "fools" (vss. 1, 16, 17, 19) and "boast" (11:12, 16, 17, 21, 30). The false apostles have boasted that they work on the same terms as Paul does (vs. 12). Paul, however, undermines their claim by boasting of things which the false apostles consider foolish: his humility (vs. 7), his labors (vs. 23), and his weakness (vs. 30).

²I feel a divine jealousy for you, for I betrothed you to Christ to present you as a pure bride to her one husband.

There is some ambiguity in verse one, depending on how the personal pronoun me or "my" (*mou*) is placed. The personal pronoun can modify **bear with**, thus meaning **bear with me**; or it can modify foolishness, meaning "my folly." The verb **I wish** (*ophelon*) is a form which is used in the New Testament to express an unrealizable wish (in English, "O that"; cf. Gal. 5:12; 1 Cor. 4:8). Here the wish is attainable, but strange, and Paul emphasizes by the word the strange nature of the request. The word **foolishness** (*aphrosunē*) is at the center of the discussion here in chapter 11, although the word occurs only in one other place in the New Testament (Mark 7:22). It seems likely that Paul's opponents, who claim for themselves eloquence (11:6), have criticized Paul for his **foolishness**. They have contrasted their wisdom with the **foolishness** of Paul. Thus in chapter 11 Paul takes the word and uses it with irony. The Corinthians listen to fools gladly enough (vs. 19). Therefore, Paul will talk like a fool and boast a little, if that behavior is necessary to get a hearing.

[2] The word for **jealousy** (*zēlos*) is also the word which is translated in other places "zeal." The word indicates the "passionate commitment to a person or a cause." Since Paul is using the figure of marriage in this passage, **jealousy** conveys the correct idea. It is not simply his own **jealousy** which Paul feels so intensely; it is a **divine jealousy.** It is the kind of **jealousy** that, according to the Old Testament, characterizes God himself. God is a "jealous God" who is provoked when Israel is unfaithful to him (Ex. 20:5). Ezekiel describes Israel's apostasy as adultery and speaks of God's marital jealousy (Ezek. 16:38; 23:25). God demands throughout the Bible the exclusive obedience of his people; anytime his people are unfaithful his **jealousy** is provoked. When Paul describes this **divine jealousy,** he implies that the church stands in the same relationship and under the same demand of God which

Israel knew in the Old Testament. Paul's **divine jealousy** may be set in contrast to the sectarian zeal of his opponents (see Gal. 4:17), who for their own purposes displayed a human jealousy.

I betrothed you to Christ. Paul seems to describe himself here as the father of the bride, through whom betrothals were made. Through Paul's missionary preaching the betrothal took place. Under these circumstances, it is natural that he should feel such **divine jealousy.** The figure of marriage is used widely in both the Old and New Testaments to describe God's relationship to his people. "The Lord has called you as a wife forsaken" (Isa. 54:6). "As the bridegroom rejoices over the bride, so shall God rejoice over you" (Isa. 62:4f.; cf. Hos. 2:7; Amos 3:2). Israel's lapses into idolatry are regarded as whoredom or as adultery (Ezek. 16:15-43; Hos. 4:10-15). In the New Testament, Christ is the bridegroom (Mark 2:19, 20) and John the Baptist is the "best man" (John 3:29). The church is the "bride" adorned for the wedding (Rev. 21:2). The marriage relationship is used in the Bible to describe God's relationship to his people because it is the deepest and most personal of relationships which men experience. Its demand for absolute loyalty is like God's demand for loyalty.

Paul, however, does not say that the marriage has taken place; the church is **betrothed.** Betrothal suggested much more to ancient people than does "engagement" today. One who was betrothed had taken vows. To break a betrothal one needed to obtain a divorce. The only difference between betrothal and marriage was that in betrothal one waited until the wedding before the marriage could be consummated. Thus Paul is saying here that the church, though **betrothed,** is yet awaiting the consummation. The "guarantee" or "engagement ring" has been received, but the marriage will not take place until the end (1:22; 5:5; Rev. 19:7).

Paul hopes to **present** (*paristēmi*) the church **to Christ,** the bridegroom, at the judgment. Paul's ambition is to **present** every man "perfect in Christ" at the judgment

³ But I am afraid that as the serpent deceived Eve by his cunning, your thoughts will be led astray from a sincere and pure devotion to Christ.

(Col. 1:28). At Ephesians 5:27, Christ will present the church to himself. The word present is often used for "presenting a sacrifice" to God (1 Cor. 8:8; 2 Cor. 4:14). Paul, as God's apostle, will present the church; it is his sacrifice to God. Sacrifices in the Old Testament were to be without any defects (Ex. 12:5; Lev. 22:19-21; Deut. 17:1). Thus Paul wants to present the church as a pure bride to the one husband, Christ. It is important that the church is to be "without spot or wrinkle," and "holy and without blemish" (Eph. 5:25f.; Rev. 14:4). This purity is maintained only by loyalty to the one husband. If they turn to "another Jesus" or "another gospel" (vs. 4), they will have become adulteresses.

[3] The church, which is in danger of becoming unfaithful, is comparable to Eve who was led astray by the serpent (Gen. 3). The serpent of Genesis 3 is not referred to as Satan or the Devil, although that identification is made in the New Testament (cf. Rev. 12:9; 20:2). In the Jewish literature before and contemporary with the New Testament, there is no general agreement on the relationship of Satan and the serpent. Some writers do not connect the serpent with Satan at all (cf. Jubilees 3:17ff.; Josephus, *Antiquities* I, 41). Other writings say that the serpent is the vessel of Satan (*Apocalypse of Moses* 16). Finally, a considerable number of rabbis equated the two (cf. *Leviticus rabba* 26 on Lev. 21:14). Wherever in the New Testament the serpent of Genesis 3 is mentioned, he is connected with Satan. Paul alludes to the story of the serpent and Eve in Romans 16:20. At 1 Timothy 2:14f. Paul derives a different lesson from Genesis 3: there Paul alludes to Eve's receptivity to Satan's arguments as an example of woman's unfitness for teaching.

The story of the serpent in Genesis 3 was for Paul a profound example of the danger that evil has, even for the good. The story was apt for the Corinthians, since they

⁴ For if some one comes and preaches another Jesus than
the one we preached, or if you receive a different spirit
from the one you received, or if you accept a different
gospel from the one you accepted, you submit to it readily
enough.

---

were in danger of accepting a different gospel (11:4) from
Satan's emissaries, who are in disguise as teachers and
ministers of righteousness (vss. 14, 15). Paul thus warns the
church here, and adds another warning for the Corinthians,
to "test" themselves at 13:5.

Paul himself finds it necessary in 2 Corinthians to
deny that he is **cunning** (*panourgia*, 4:2; 12:6), a quality
which Paul ascribes to the devil in 6:11. By being **cunning**,
Paul's opponents are proving themselves to be Satan's messengers in disguise (vss. 14, 15). Because the church
listens to enticing arguments, their **thoughts** are in danger
of being **led astray.** God is a jealous God, and he will
allow no competitors. To turn to "another Jesus" (vs. 4)
would be the same as to turn from their **sincere** or "single
minded" (*haplotēs*) devotion to Christ. The word translated here **sincere** (*haplotēs*) is translated "simplicity" in
the KJV. It describes one who is "wholehearted" or un-
divided in his attention. "Simplicity" carries a connotation to modern ears which does not represent what Paul
has in mind. He has in mind a "singleminded" devotion
to Christ. Christ will allow no sharing of affections; no
one can serve "two masters" (Matt. 6:24). The RSV has
the words **and pure devotion** (*hagnotētos*), which the KJV
omits. The words are omitted in many old manuscripts;
yet the weight of manuscript tradition, including the early
papyrus, p⁴⁶, favors the words. The **pure devotion** is a
reference to the chastity which is necessary for the bride
of Christ to maintain.

[4] Paul here tells what form this seduction takes. He
clearly indicates that the message of the intruders is not
the true gospel. At 11:1 Paul asked the church to "bear
with" (*anechesthe*) his foolishness; at verse 4 he accuses
the Corinthians: whenever someone comes preaching a

false message, you submit to it (*anechesthe*), using the same word. Paul is asking the church to give him as much consideration as they give his opponents. Moffatt adds the words in his translation which the statement implies: "Why not put up with me?" The KJV, following a different manuscript tradition, makes all of verse 4 entirely hypothetical ("ye might well bear with him"). The best manuscript tradition, however (and indeed the context of the passage), shows that this is not a hypothetical question. Thus the RSV rendering: you submit (or "bear with") it readily.

The subject of Paul's preaching has been given succinctly at 4:5. He preaches "Jesus Christ as Lord." At 1 Corinthians 1:23, Paul's preaching is said to center in "Christ crucified." It is noteworthy that Paul virtually always prefers to call Jesus by the descriptive titles "Lord" and "Christ"; his opponents prefer the earthly name Jesus. Jesus refers to the human, earthly figure. "Lord" and "Christ" are titles given to Jesus as a result of the cross and resurrection (Acts 2:36; Phil. 2:11). We know from 11:22 that his opponents were Jewish Christians; their interest was in the earthly appearances of Jesus in the flesh. It is possible that their claim to authenticity as apostles was derived from their acquaintance with the earthly Jesus. How can this be another Jesus? For Paul, Jesus was the crucified and suffering savior whose death was necessary for the reconciliation of the world (5:19). Those who preached another Jesus saw him as a revealer like Moses (cf. 3:7-18), as a great teacher, but not as a lowly, suffering Messiah.

What is at stake is the validity of Paul's ministry. If the opponents are correct in their view of Jesus as an eloquent teacher and revealer, then they are true apostles, and Paul's "weakness" (10:10) and suffering (4:7-12) is senseless. If, however, Paul is correct in preaching the cross of Christ, then his sufferings validate his apostleship.

The New Testament speaks frequently of "receiving the Spirit" (John 7:39; 14:17; 20:22; Rom. 8:15), which is the Holy Spirit. But it is not the Holy Spirit which one

⁵ I think that I am not in the least inferior to these superlative apostles. ⁶ Even if I am unskilled in speaking, I am
not in knowledge; in every way we have made this plain
to you in all things.

---

receives if he accepts the teachings of those who preach
another Jesus; it is a different spirit. Paul's opponents
have emphasized their gifts of the Spirit (cf. comments on
5:13; cf. 11:6; 12:1-8). Paul's answer is that one does not
preach a different message and receive the same Spirit,
for the Spirit is the Spirit of Christ (Rom. 8:9). Whatever
spirit they may boast about is not the Holy Spirit. To
preach another Jesus or another spirit is to preach another
gospel.

Paul, in Galatians 1:6-9, accuses the Galatians of turn-
ing to a "different gospel" which is in fact no gospel at
all. The different gospel there is the message of the Judaizers. Here it is the message which preaches a Jesus without a cross. There is but one gospel—the message of
Christ crucified and risen.

[5] What is the connection between verses 4 and 5?
Paul, by being loyal to Christ and by accepting his cross,
has validated his apostleship. The opponents have compared themselves to Paul (10:12), and have declared Paul
to be inferior. Apostles is used here in a general sense of
travelling missionaries (see comments on 1:1). Paul's description of them as superlative apostles is, of course,
sarcastic. At verse 13, he says that they merely disguise
themselves as "apostles of Christ." The superiority may have
been thought to derive from their personal acquaintance
with the earthly Jesus. Some have thought that the opponents were claiming superiority based on their contacts
with the Jerusalem church (cf. Gal. 2:12).

[6] Verse 6 gives the particular charge that Paul's opponents have made against him. It is implied that these
"superlative apostles" were able speakers, a gift which Paul
never claims for himself (cf. 1 Cor. 2:4; see 2 Cor. 10:10
and discussion there). The word for unskilled is *idiōtēs*,
which has the usual meaning "uneducated." The word is

⁷ Did I commit a sin in abasing myself so that you might be exalted, because I preached God's gospel without cost to you?

---

used in 1 Corinthians 14:16 for one who does not have the gift of tongues or the interpretation of tongues. Paul's opponents, who display their spiritual gifts, infer that Paul does not have God's Spirit because he does not display his gift of tongues (a gift Paul does have, according to 1 Cor. 14:18). According to 13:3, they go so far as to demand proof that Christ even speaks through Paul. Paul's response here is that, although he is **unskilled in speaking,** he is not remiss in other talents, i.e., in **knowledge** (*gnōsis*). The **knowledge** which Paul claims here is no factual information. It is a **knowledge** of God (cf. 2:14; 4:6; 10:5). This **knowledge** is a recognition and acknowledgment of God; it is a personal relationship with God (or Christ) whereby Paul has come to "know him" (see Phil. 3:8). Paul has **made this plain** (*phanerōsantes*) by his proper conduct and by his sufferings as an apostle (4:10, 11). The expressions **in every way** (*en panti*) and **in all things** (*en pasin*) are used frequently in 2 Corinthians (4:8; 6:4; 7:5) to show the extent of Paul's labors. He has left no grounds for suspicion of his ministry. **In every way** he has lived in a way compatible with the message which he preached.

[7] In 1 Corinthians 9:3-14, Paul discusses at length his right to obtain pay for his preaching, a right which he did not make use of (1 Cor. 9:12). Others had the right, and did accept support (1 Cor. 9:12). Now in 2 Corinthians, Paul's opponents had demanded the right to accept support by "preying" on the church. This right of the itinerant preacher came under considerable abuse in the second century, causing the church to restrict its giving. The writer of the *Didache* (early second century) says: "When an Apostle goes forth let him accept nothing but bread till he reach his night's lodging; but if he ask for money, he is a false prophet." In verse 7, they evidently conclude that Paul's renunciation of support was a sign

⁸ I robbed other churches by accepting support from them in order to serve you.

---

of weakness, that Paul was not very secure in his position (see also comments on 2:17). Here in verses 7-11, Paul answers the charge that he sinned by not accepting support. This support seems to have been a very important concern for the opponents.

Paul has been accused of **sin** in not accepting support. Paul uses the word in an unusual way here; probably he is using the word in the sense which his opponents had employed. The word for **sin** (*hamartia*) means "missing the mark." Paul generally uses the word with reference to man's condition as a sinner; seldom, if ever, does he speak elsewhere of an individual sin, as he does here. All men entered this condition of sin through Adam, the representative of mankind (Rom. 5:12-19). Sin is a power which "reigns" in man (Rom. 5:21). Here Paul speaks of a particular offense or **sin** of which he has been accused. Paul's **abasing** refers to his renunciation of support. They are **exalted** by Paul's activity to the glory of Christ.

[8] Paul let other churches support him while he preached and ministered to the Corinthians. His strong feeling is expressed in the statement that he **robbed other churches.** What Paul tells us here is confirmed in Philippians 4:15. Because of his cordial relationship with that church, he departed from his rule of not accepting support. Paul **robbed** them by accepting funds which they could have used. The word for **support** (*opsōnion*) does not imply any abundance of funds. The word means "maintenance support." It is used mostly for the payment to a soldier. The word is used in 1 Corinthians 9:7, where Paul says, "Who serves as a soldier at his own expense?" Paul shows by his use of this word that he thinks of himself as God's soldier who has received ration pay from the Macedonians.

The end product of Paul's acceptance of support was **in order to serve** (literally, "for your service"). The very thing about which Paul is being accused was for their

⁹ And when I was with you and was in want, I did not
burden any one, for my needs were supplied by the
brethren who came from Macedonia. So I refrained and
will refrain from burdening you in any way. ¹⁰ As the truth
of Christ is in me, this boast of mine shall not be silenced
in the regions of Achaia.

---

benefit. He did not want his "ministry" or "service" dis-
credited (see 6:3), and his intent in not accepting support
was to be sure that no one could accuse him of being
mercenary.

[9] Paul has already described the generosity of the
Macedonians in 8:1, 2. Evidently, when Paul first came to
Corinth, he was in want. His work of tentmaking may not
have provided for his needs (see Acts 18:3). Even then he
did not burden any one (cf. 1 Thess. 2:9; 2 Thess. 3:8).
The brethren who came from Macedonia supplied this lack.
These brethren were either Silas and Timothy (Acts
18:5), who brought help sent by Macedonian churches, or
Macedonian messengers whose names we do not know.
Earlier, when Paul was in Thessalonica, and later when he
was in prison in Rome, the Philippians sent gifts to Paul
(Phil. 4:16, 18). It was such experiences as these that could
cause Paul to say, "My God will supply every need of yours"
(Phil. 4:19).

[10] Because Paul's truthfulness has been questioned,
he takes a solemn oath: As the truth of Christ is in me.
This solemn statement has the purpose of giving weight to
Paul's statement. It is not uncommon for Paul to defend
his truthfulness with statements of this nature (see Rom.
9:1, "I speak the truth in Christ"). Just as elsewhere, Paul
says that Christ is in him (Gal. 2:20) and that the Spirit
is in him (Rom. 8:9f.), here he claims that the truth of
Christ is in him. Here and at 1 Corinthians 9:15, Paul
points to his unwillingness to accept financial support as a
grounds of boasting. This boast from Paul sounds strange,
since Paul elsewhere says that because one is saved by
grace, boasting is excluded (Rom. 3:27). Frequently
throughout 2 Corinthians Paul has rejected the boasting

¹¹ And why? Because I do not love you? God knows I do!

¹² And what I do I will continue to do, in order to undermine the claim of those who would like to claim that in their boasted mission they work on the same terms as we do. ¹³ For such men are false apostles, deceitful workmen, disguising themselves as the apostles of Christ.

---

which characterizes his opponents (3:1; 5:12; 10:12, 18). Yet in chapters 10—13 Paul boasts continually (10:8, 13, 15; 11:16, 21, 30; 12:1). Paul has been forced into his boasting by his opponents, who claim that they work on the same terms as he does (11:12). They boast of worldly things (11:18); Paul boasts of his weakness (11:30). Thus when he boasts that he has not accepted support, he is not showing that he is greater than others; he is showing his weakness (11:30). The **regions of Achaia** include the district of which Corinth was the chief city (see 1:1).

[11] Paul's adversaries have said that Paul's refusal to accept the support was that he did not care sufficiently for them. The charge may sound strange, but Paul's opponents seem to have felt that there was something in this support more important than to have sustenance. The church had a duty to provide it, and when it did not, it was remiss in its duties. Thus for them, when Paul did not accept support, it was proof that he did not **love** them. **God knows** that he does.

[12] According to verse 20, Paul's opponents lived at the expense of the church. They find it necessary to discredit Paul because they will be compared with him. Paul, by refusing support, seeks to **undermine** any claim they might make to a favorable comparison to him. If he accepted support he would be doing his opponents a favor, verifying their claims to be apostles like Paul. But by refusing support, he removes their pretext for accepting money.

[13] Paul's reason for not accepting support was that he wanted to keep the line between himself and his intruders drawn clearly. The language here is strong. His

156

¹⁴ And no wonder, for even Satan disguises himself as an angel of light. ¹⁵ So it is not strange if his servants also disguise themselves as servants of righteousness. Their end will correspond to their deeds.

---

opponents are **false apostles** (*pseudapostoloi*). At 11:5, he has already called them "superlative apostles." They are **false** because their message is false (11:4); they were not commissioned by Christ, since they do not even preach him correctly. They are proved false by their methods: they are **deceitful workmen** (*ergatai doloi*). The word *ergatēs* ("workman") is often applied to disciples (cf. Matt. 10:10; Luke 10:7). The disciple is to be, in contrast to these **deceitful workmen,** "blameless and innocent" (see Phil. 2:15). Paul frequently appeals to his integrity in his work as evidence that his message is valid (cf. 4:2; 6:3ff.; 2:17). It seems to be axiomatic for Paul that the true disciple of Christ imitates his Lord (cf. 6:3ff.; 4:10-11); **deceitful workers** cannot be from Christ. They disguise themselves as **apostles of Christ,** which they are not.

[14] The charge against his opponents is particularly sharp here. The opponents have proved themselves by their methods not to be Christ's apostles but apostles of **Satan.** That they act with deceit is **no** cause for **wonder.** That is the way of **Satan** and his servants. Paul has already referred to Satan's act of deceiving Eve (11:3); Satan's messengers continue these methods. The reference to Satan's disguise may be a reminiscence of an old Jewish legend that Satan once took the form of an **angel of light** and joined other angels in singing praises to God. Eve in the garden is said to have caught sight of him in this guise as he "bent over the wall." Paul's point is that evil can counterfeit goodness.

[15] Just as Satan deceived Eve, Paul says that Satan's **servants** are trying to deceive the church. A servant resembles his master. Paul resembles the lowliness of Jesus. His opponents claim to be **servants** of Christ (11:23), but their actions prove that they resemble Satan more.

Paul uses the word servant (*diakonos*) and related

16 I repeat, let no one think me foolish; but even if you do, accept me as a fool, so that I too may boast a little.

---

words like "ministry" (*diakonia*) more in 2 Corinthians than any other book (cf. 3:7, 8, 9; 4:1; 5:18; 6:4). No doubt these extended discussions of his ministry or service are made necessary by Paul's opponents. These opponents have called themselves "servants of Christ" (11:23) and **servants of righteousness.** Because of the high position these opponents apply to Moses (see 3:17-18), it is possible that they consider themselves simultaneously to be "servants of Christ" and "servants of Moses." Paul argues in chapter 3 that his own ministry is superior to the ministry of Moses because Paul's is a ministry of the new covenant, a ministry of the Spirit (3:6), and a ministry of reconciliation (5:18). When Paul argues the temporary nature of Moses' ministry, he probably has in mind those ministers **of righteousness** who extol Moses' ministry, and model themselves after him. It is Paul's ministry, not Moses' ministry, that is a "ministry of righteousness" (3:9).

That God renders to every man "according to his deeds" is stated in the Old Testament as God's criterion of judgment (Jer. 17:10; Ps. 61:5). In the New Testament the same principle is frequently stated (cf. Rom. 2:6; 2 Tim. 4:14; Rev. 2:23; cf. 2 Cor. 5:10). The **end** (*telos*) or "outcome" to which Paul refers can certainly refer to God's final judgment, as at 5:10. But Paul may have in mind something more immediate. He is about to come to Corinth, at which time they will be put to the "test" (13:5); those who fail the test will not be "spared" (13:2), i.e., Paul will inflict some kind of punishment of them. Thus the **end** may refer to the outcome of Paul's visit with them. Their punishment will **correspond to their deeds.**

Paul's Labor and Hardships, 11:16—12:10

[16] In the remainder of the chapter Paul at last enters into a detailed comparison of his own claims to be an apostle of Christ with those put forward by his opponents. Returning now to the request of verse 1, Paul repeats his

¹⁷ (**What I am saying I say not with the Lord's authority but as a fool, in this boastful confidence;** ¹⁸ **since many boast of worldly things, I too will boast.**) ¹⁹ **For you gladly bear with fools, being wise yourselves!**

---

original plea that they pardon him for boasting. "Boasting" is the key word in the entire section, 11:16—12:10.

The subject of being **foolish** is mentioned again (see vs. 1). Paul equates a certain kind of boasting with foolishness (vs. 21); it is the boasting, which his opponents do, and it is concerned with outward position (vs. 22). Paul knows that self-boasting is **foolish**, since no man who is saved by God's grace can boast. But the opponents have challenged Paul's authority, and have boasted of their superiority over Paul. Therefore, they have forced Paul to be a **fool** (12:11), having made it necessary for Paul himself to **boast** of outward things (vs. 22; 12:1-6). Here Paul asks them to accept him as a **fool**, so that he could **boast**. He has been forced to argue on their terms, the only terms they understand.

[17,18] Verse 17 does not imply that Paul is disobeying a command from the Lord. He has simply been forced to argue from the point of view of his opponents, and not from the Lord's perspective, in order to answer his opponents. He is a **fool** for boasting of **worldly things** (*kata sarka*, "according to the flesh"). The false teachers have accused Paul of being "worldly" (10:2); but it is they who **boast of worldly things.** These **worldly things** are listed in verse 22.

Paul knows that the Jewish descent of which the opponents boast is a worldly matter and not a matter for boasting. Indeed, he has counted all of these things as "loss" for the sake of Christ (Phil. 3:7). Yet, he says, **I too will boast** of Hebrew descent (11:22), achievements, and visions from the Lord (12:1). He will **boast** of these things in order to refute his opponents' claim to superiority.

[19] The reason Paul argues here in "foolish" terms is that experience has shown at Corinth that they **bear with fools** (see 11:4, 20). It is the fool who gets a hearing at

159

20 For you bear it if a man makes slaves of you, or preys upon you, or takes advantage of you, or puts on airs, or strikes you in the face. 21 To my shame, I must say, we were too weak for that!

Corinth. Here Paul uses irony to make his point. The Corinthians are so **wise** (*phronimoi*) that they **bear with fools.** They are not wise in the usual sense of the word, but **wise** in their own estimation (cf. Rom. 11:25; 12:16; 1 Cor. 4:8, 10). Their wisdom is only a worldly wisdom, which causes them to appreciate these worldly opponents.

[20] Verse 20 lists the offenses of Paul's opponents. **A man** is literally "anyone" (*tis*). All such troublemakers are included. They **make slaves** (*katadouloi*) of the Corinthians. This conduct is in contrast to Paul, who calls himself "slave" of all (1 Cor. 9:19). Nor do they imitate Jesus, who came "in the form of a slave" (Phil. 2:7). They **prey** (*katesthiein*) on the church. The word in Greek means to "devour" or "eat up." Here Paul uses the word with the meaning "to exploit." When they demand funds, they prey on the church. They **take advantage** (*lambanein*) of the church. Literally, they "take" the church by placing on them an excessive burden (12:16), and by living at their expense. **To put on airs** is literally "to lift up oneself" (*epairo*). It is a human pride that exalts itself in defiance of God and man. The expression **strikes you in the face** probably does not refer to any physical treatment. The expression is often used figuratively for rough treatment (cf. 1 Cor. 4:11; 9:27). Paul says ironically, you put up with all of that; surely you can tolerate a little boasting from me.

[21] Paul refers ironically to the offenses of his opponents. They have charged Paul with "weakness" (10:10), which they said made him incapable of leading. Paul takes up their charge and uses it against them: he was too **weak** to take advantage of the Corinthians as his opponents had done. Ironically he says, What a **shame!** Paul's opponents are fools in boasting of their Jewish descent. But to assure

**But whatever any one dares to boast of—I am speaking
as a fool—I also dare to boast of that. [22] Are they Hebrews?
So am I. Are they Israelites? So am I. Are they descendants
of Abraham? So am I.**

---

his readers that the false teachers have no advantage, Paul
will boast on the level of a **fool.**

[22] The boasting, repeatedly mentioned from 10:8 on,
now begins. In every respect, Paul can match the Jewish
standing of his opponents, who had boasted of their Jewish
descent. Paul's response to them is reminiscent of his
response to the opponents in Philippians 3:2-6. All of the
words for boasting in verse 22 suggest the Jewishness of
Paul's opponents. The word **Hebrews** is not entirely clear.
The word is used only three times in the New Testament
(cf. Acts 6:1; Phil. 3:5). In Acts 6:1, Luke says that there
was a dispute between the Hellenists and the Hebrews.
It is possible that these Hebrews are Palestinians who speak
Aramaic, as opposed to Greek-speaking Hellenists; understood this way, their conflict arose over language barriers.
More likely is the view that the Hebrews and the Hellenists
represented two different attitudes toward the law. According to this view, the Hebrews held to a stricter interpretation of the law. At Philippians 3:5, Paul calls himself a "Hebrew of Hebrews." His reference there may be
to the fact that he spoke Hebrew, as well as to the fact
that he had not been "hellenized" while growing up in
a Greek city. His religious orthodoxy is stressed in the
context. When Paul calls himself a **Hebrew** here at verse
22, he is speaking of his completely Jewish background and
ancestry; he is no proselyte. He is a Jew in the full sense
of the word. He, unlike many Jews who lived in Greek
culture, had preserved the Aramaic language of Palestine
(Acts 22:2). As a Hebrew, he held to the strict observance
of the law. The word **Israelites** suggests not only national
origins, but religious convictions also. One could be a
Hebrew by descent without being an Israelite. An Israelite

²³ **Are they servants of Christ? I am a better one—I am talking like a madman—with far greater labors, far more imprisonments, with countless beatings, and often near death.**

---

is one who has remained true to his covenant with God (cf. Rom. 9:4; 11:1). Paul is of the seed of **Abraham;** he is no proselyte. Paul is fully Jewish in every sense: in religion and in nationality. He knows that this fact means nothing before God; but since it is important to the Corinthians, he boasts about his Jewishness.

[23] The false teachers claim to be **servants of Christ. Servants** here is comparable to "apostles" (vs. 13); the false teachers use both titles for themselves. The reason Paul has defended his service or ministry is that they have given themselves the title **servants of Christ.** They base their claim on their knowledge of the earthly Jesus (5:16; 11:4), upon their Jewish descent (11:22), and upon their impressive manner and spiritual gifts (12:1ff.). They have no right to call themselves **servants of Christ** according to Paul. Their model for service has not been Christ, the "suffering servant"; instead, their model has been "another Jesus" (11:4), one who was mighty in word and deed and Spirit-filled. One is a servant **of Christ** only when he has been appointed by the mercy of God (4:1) and when he imitates the weakness of Christ (6:4ff.; 4:10-11). Thus in verses 23-29, Paul is a **better** servant because he has endured suffering. The recital of his hardships are a commentary on his words at 4:10, that he always carried in his body the death of Jesus. In his suffering, he was following the words of his Lord, who demanded, "Take up your cross" (Mark 8:34). That is the conduct which marks true **servants.** The details recorded in 23-27 indicate how many experiences of this kind are unrecorded elsewhere. Paul only mentions these experiences in self-defense.

Paul's necessary boasting elicits from him the renewed protest that he is **talking like a madman.** Even if he must boast to defend himself, he finds the task distasteful. The

²⁴ **Five times I have received at the hands of the Jews
the forty lashes less one.**

---

language of fools is the only language they understand,
and so he continues his boasting.

As an apostle, Paul had the right to accept support and
avoid **labors** (*kopoi*); his opponents have not distinguished
themselves by **labors**. Paul knows that his **labors** for Christ
are exhausting (see 1 Cor. 15:10), yet these **labors** are
his grounds for boasting. **Imprisonments** are mentioned
here and at 6:5 as a validation of his service to Christ.
Only one specific imprisonment is recorded in Acts before
the writing of 2 Corinthians: the one at Philippi (Acts
16:23). The **beatings** are further described in verses 24, 25.
Often near death is literally, "in many deaths." According
to Jewish thought, one is in the dominion of **death** when
one is seized by various diseases and disorders (Héring,
p. 84). Paul had numerous narrow escapes from death; one
such incident is recorded at 1:8, where he "despaired of
life itself."

[24] Here the beatings of verse 23 are given in detail.
These **five** incidents are unrecorded elsewhere. Deuteronomy 25:1-3 prescribed the penalty of forty lashes. Since
the law said that the number must not exceed forty, the
practice arose of giving one less in order to avoid all
danger of violating this rule. Paul is the earliest witness
to this practice, but Josephus and later Jewish witnesses
confirm it. This punishment was so severe that it sometimes caused death. It was administered with leather
thongs, two thirds of the lashes given across the back, one
third across the chest. Evidently, this punishment was administered for religious offenses to the Jews, even outside
Palestine. The fact that Paul received this punishment
several times indicates that throughout his ministry there
was no final separation between the church and the synagogue. This constant interaction between Paul and the synagogue is confirmed throughout Acts (cf. Acts 9:2; 18:8,
12-17; 19:8ff.; 22:5; 26:9-11).

²⁵ **Three times I have been beaten with rods; once I
was stoned. Three times I have been shipwrecked; a night
and a day I have been adrift at sea;** ²⁶ **on frequent journeys,
in danger from rivers, danger from robbers, danger from
my own people, danger from Gentiles, danger in the city,
danger in the wilderness, danger at sea, danger from false
brethren;**

---

[25] Beatings **with rods** was a Roman punishment,
usually administered by city magistrates. Acts tells of one
beating at Philippi (Acts 16:22-23). Since Paul was a
Roman citizen by birth, this punishment was illegal. In
Acts 22:24, Paul's Roman citizenship prevented such a
beating. No explanation is given as to why Paul's Roman
citizenship did not have the same effect at Philippi (Acts
16:25-38).

The stoning is briefly mentioned in Acts 14:19 as the
result of a Jewish riot. This form of punishment was the
obligatory punishment among Jews for certain religious
crimes, such as false prophecy and blasphemy (cf. Lev. 20;
Deut. 13 and 17; Ex. 19).

The three shipwrecks are not known to the book of
Acts. But a fourth took place in Acts on Paul's voyage to
Rome (Acts 27). During one of these shipwrecks, Paul
spent twenty-four hours "in the deep," i.e., in the open sea.
It must be supposed that Paul saved himself there, as in
Acts 27, by clinging to some of the wreckage.

[26] The **frequent journeys** (*hodoiporiai*) are literally,
"journeys on roads." They are in contrast to the sea
voyages of verse 25. Even during the Pax Romana of Paul's
day, when Roman rule made travel safer than before,
journeys could be perilous. The **danger from rivers** must
refer to the absence of bridges or easily negotiable fords.
The **robbers** are highwaymen or pirates who were a threat
in remote areas. Dangers from Paul's **countrymen** and
dangers from **Gentiles** are mentioned throughout Acts
(Acts 14:19ff.; 20:3; 19:23). **False brethren** (*pseudadel-
phoi*) are mentioned here and at Galatians 2:4. Paul may

²⁷ in toil and hardship, through many a sleepless night, in hunger and thirst, often without food, in cold and exposure. ²⁸ And, apart from other things, there is the daily pressure upon me of my anxiety for all the churches. ²⁹ Who is weak, and I am not weak? Who is made to fall, and I am not indignant?

---

have in mind Judaizers like those discussed in Galatians; or he may mean simply "mischief makers."

[27] New categories of Paul's ordeals are now listed. Here he does not discuss specific dangers; he is more concerned with the sum of his experiences. **Toil and hardship** is a phrase already used in 1 Thessalonians 2:9 and 2 Thessalonians 3:8. The phrase describes Paul's heavy load of preaching and manual labor (see 1 Cor. 4:12). The **many a sleepless night,** mentioned already at 6:5 (*agrupnia* is translated there "watching") were caused by his anxiety for the churches (vs. 28). The **hunger** and **thirst** and periods **without food** were brought about by unavoidable lack of food and not by voluntary fasting. Hard journeys could also result in unavoidable **cold and exposure.**

[28] To the distresses listed in verses 27, 28 is the **daily pressure** (*epistasis*) or "tension" of his responsibility for the churches. Paul's burden does not consist in outward deprivation alone; a part of his heavy burden is the **pressure** which his responsibility causes. Paul never forgets the churches he has founded. The **pressure** comes in the form of **anxiety** (*merimna*) for the churches. **Anxiety** in the form of earthly "cares" is condemned in the New Testament because it betrays a lack of trust in God (Matt. 6:25-34; Phil. 4:6; 1 Peter 5:7). But **anxiety** on behalf of others is to be commended: "that the members may have the same care for one another" (1 Cor. 12:25). This **anxiety** of Paul's is seen in his frequent correspondence with churches, his visits, and the messengers he sends. A good view of this **anxiety** is provided at 7:5. **All** includes the Corinthian church, but it is a reminder that Paul has other churches in his care (cf. 2:12-13).

[29] Paul experiences complete empathy for his congre-

⁰ If I must boast, I will boast of the things that show my weakness. ³¹ The God and Father of the Lord Jesus, he who is blessed for ever, knows that I do not lie. ³² At Damascus, the governor under King Aretas guarded the city of Damascus in order to seize me, ³³ but I was let down in a basket through a window in the wall, and escaped his hands.

---

gations. The weakness about which he has been criticized is really a deep concern for his churches. Those who have not experienced this weakness are not concerned about them and cannot be faithful servants of Christ. When someone stumbles or is **made to fall** (*skandalizetai*), Paul is **indignant** (literally, "on fire").

[30] The precise meaning of Paul's **boast** at verse 18 is given here. The boasting in external matters is not legitimate. The **weakness** of which he has been accused (10:10) is the only subject for boasting, for it is in **weakness** that Paul demonstrates his likeness to Christ, who was "crucified in weakness" (13:4).

Verse 30 is an apt summary of all that has been said in verses 23-29. All that has been said there has been to demonstrate Paul's **weakness**. It is this **weakness** which proves that Paul is more like Christ than his opponents are, and thus "a better servant of Christ" than they (see 11:23).

[31] Paul is concerned here that his recital of his sufferings in 11:23-29 may be contested. Verse 31 is a solemn oath, asserting the truthfulness of what has been said. For similar oaths, see 1:18, 23; 11:10.

[32,33] Verses 32, 33 seem quite out of place here. The doxology at verse 31 leaves the impression that Paul has completed his recital of sufferings. The change is so abrupt here that some have suggested that verses 32, 33 were a later addition. The change is abrupt, but this characteristic is not unusual for Paul; and the story is an apt illustration of the kind of ordeals listed in 23-29. Strachan (p. 28) has suggested that the story of Paul's escape from Damascus

¹ I must boast; there is nothing to be gained by it, but I will go on to visions and revelations of the Lord.

---

had been circulated by Paul's opponents in order to dramatize Paul's weakness and expose him to ridicule. If that conjecture is correct, Paul brings up the episode in order to set the record straight. What to Paul's opponents was a ridiculous situation was to Paul an example of God's mercy providing deliverance despite his human weakness. Never did Paul feel more helpless than at this time; yet this event in the beginning of Paul's ministry taught him that God's deliverance comes in impossible situations.

The story which Paul relates has a parallel account in Acts 9:23-25. One difference is that in Acts it is the Jews who plot to kill Paul, whereas here it is the governor under **King Aretas** who instigates the plot. It is not unlikely that the Jews conspired with the king. Luke consistently emphasizes the Jewish hostility in Acts (13:46, 50; 14:19; 17:5), and thus his emphasis on Jewish hostility in this story is not surprising.

Aretas was, no doubt, Aretas IV, head of a Nabataean kingdom (east of Palestine), who reigned from 9 B.C. to A.D. 39 (see vol. 1, p. 60). It is possible that he captured Damascus in A.D. 34, a town which had been in Roman hands since 63 B.C. Thus Paul's flight was probably somewhere between A.D. 34 and 39.

[1] Paul begins a new section of his "boastful speech" in chapter 12. In 11:23-29 Paul appeals to his sufferings as proof of his apostleship. His opponents, however, extol ecstasy and visions (see comments on 5:13) as proof that one has the Spirit. This extreme emphasis on ecstatic experiences has already been the subject for Paul's discussion at 1 Corinthians 12 and 14. There Paul claimed the gift for himself (1 Cor. 14:18); nevertheless these gifts are useless unless they edify the church (1 Cor. 14:19). Paul never makes a display of his gifts; they are no grounds for boasting, because they are gifts from the Lord.

Here, as at 11:16ff., Paul is apologetic about his boasting. He would never have appealed to these experiences if his opponents had not forced him to. They have accused him of being "worldly" and therefore not "spiritual" (10:2), of making his plans in a worldly way and not by the direction of the Spirit (1:12). Paul now relates these ecstatic experiences in order to prove to his detractors that he does have the Spirit.

The theme of boasting occurs throughout this chapter (vss. 1, 5, 6, 9). Yet Paul's regret that he **must boast** is plain throughout, and is stressed here. His preference, to admit his own weakness and rely on God's grace, is repeated frequently (vss. 5, 6, 9, 10). The Greek manuscripts vary slightly on the precise wording of verse 1. One may notice that the sense of **I must boast** is not given in the KJV; the reason is that the Greek word **must** (*dei*) is not found in some manuscripts; nevertheless, the best manuscripts support the reading of the RSV, **I must boast.** Paul has been forced to boast (vs. 11) by his opponents. The words **there is nothing to be gained by it** do not imply that Paul can achieve nothing with this boasting he is about to do; otherwise he would not bother. He is simply expressing his distaste for the whole business of boasting, forced on him by his opponents.

That Paul did not like to boast about his spiritual experiences is well proved by the fact that the experiences related in verse 1-4 sound so unlike Paul. Although Paul wrote many letters covering different aspects of Christian experience, these **visions and revelations** certainly have no prominent place. We notice here, as at 1 Corinthians 14:18, 19, that Paul had the gifts but did not make much of them. In 1 Corinthians 13, these gifts are clearly less important than love.

Visions (*optasia*) and **revelations** (*apokalupseis*) are two ways that divine communication is made in the Bible. Revelation, meaning literally "uncovering," is the more general category. Man's native intelligence is incapable of grasping the ways and purposes of God; the only way a man can understand God's purpose is by revelation. Paul is aware that some Christians have a gift of revelation (1

² I know a man in Christ who fourteen years ago was caught up to the third heaven—whether in the body or out of the body I do not know, God knows. ³ And I know that this man was caught up into Paradise—whether in the body or out of the body I do not know, God knows—

Cor. 14:6, 26, 30), a gift which he claims here for himself (see Gal. 2:2). A vision is a type of revelation (see Luke 1:22 of Zacharias' vision; cf. Acts 18:9; 22:14f., for such experiences by Paul, though described in different words). Since **visions** and **revelations** are not two separate experiences, Paul is claiming to have seen "visions and other revelations." He is not referring to his experience on the Damascus road, although that experience is called a vision (Acts 26:19) and a revelation (Gal. 1:12) elsewhere. The plural form of these **visions** indicates an occurrence that took place more than once. Paul appears here to be talking about a gift of the Spirit (cf. 1 Cor. 14:6, 26, 30) which he has from the Lord. We do not know what took place in these great experiences. It is possible he means that on such occasions he saw the living Lord, Jesus, as he did on the Damascus road (see 1 Cor. 9:1; cf. also Stephen's experience, Acts 7:56); but **of the Lord** can just as easily refer to experiences brought about by the Lord. Perhaps his experience is similar to John's, who was "in the Spirit on the Lord's day" (Rev. 1:10). Whatever the nature of these visions was, Paul refers to them in order to meet his opponents on their own ground. If they claim to have superior spiritual experiences, he can make the same claim.

[2,3] As verse 7 shows, Paul was the **man in Christ.** It was not uncommon among Jewish people for a man to refer to himself in the third person (see vs. 5). One can compare those passages where Jesus uses "Son of man" as a substitute for "I" (see Matt. 8:20). The expression **in Christ** is used here to mean a Christian. To be **in Christ** is to be in his body, the church (cf. 5:17; Eph. 4:4; Rom. 12:4, 5). One who is **in Christ** has died with him and has been raised with him (see Rom. 6:4ff.).

Paul claims to have been **caught up,** either **in the body or out of the body,** into the **third heaven** (vs. 2) or **Paradise** (vs. 3). Opinion is divided among scholars as to whether Paul in verses 2 and 3 is describing two places and two experiences, or whether in verse 3 Paul is restating what he has said in verse 2. The verbal repetition in verse 3 seems to indicate that the same experience is meant. Jewish writings spoke of more than one heaven. Some rabbis spoke of three heavens: the first heaven, the sky; the second, the heavenly ocean; and the third, God's throne. Other rabbis, however, spoke of seven heavens. Thus it is impossible to know whether Paul's heavenly journey was to the highest level or not. **Paradise** (vs. 3) is the place of the righteous departed (see Luke 23:43). A few Jewish documents located **Paradise** in the **third heaven** (*Apocalypse of Moses* 40:2; *Slavonic Enoch* 8:1), and so it seems further apparent that verses 2 and 3 are describing the same experience. According to Revelation 2:7, it is only the elect who will enjoy **Paradise** at the end time. Paul has thus had the privilege of being able to enter in advance, even though his journey was temporary. According to verse 7, there was an "abundance of revelations" in which he has had profound emotional and spiritual experiences; the frequency of Paul's great experiences is confirmed by Acts (18:9; 22:17; 23:11). But he has in mind here one great experience that was more powerful than any other. Thus he remembers a specific moment **fourteen years ago,** i.e., around A.D. 40 or 41.

The experience was so profound that Paul does not remember whether he was **in the body or out of the body.** He supposes that either he was transported bodily into heaven or that for a period his soul left the body. The question of how this experience took place is only an academic question for Paul. The important thing is what happened: an experience that took place **fourteen years ago** but still remains fresh in his mind. Paul's experience was not one that he could stimulate in himself or "turn on" at will. He was **caught up** or "grasped." The Lord, and not Paul, was the power at work.

⁴ and he heard things that cannot be told, which man may
not utter. ⁵ On behalf of this man I will boast, but on
my own behalf I will not boast, except of my weaknesses. ⁶ Though if I wish to boast, I shall not be a fool,
for I shall be speaking the truth. But I refrain from it,
so that no one may think more of me than he sees in me
or hears from me.

---

[4] Those things which **cannot be told** (literally, "un-
utterable utterances") do not refer to experiences that
one cannot express in human language. The expression
which man may not utter means it is forbidden for a man
to utter them. The experience was too sacred for Paul to
relate. Paul may be here deliberately contrasting himself
to those opponents who boast of their experiences.

What is impressive here is how little Paul emphasizes
such a great experience. Paul is very unlike any of the
Hellenistic mystics and Jewish apocalyptic writers and
prophets who were known for their visions. Paul's experience of the power of God is not limited to visions; it
is in his weakness, in his daily hardships, that he finds
the power of God always available.

[5] Such visions and revelations were a great privilege
and support to Paul in his hardship and suffering. They
will silence the criticism of those who claim that his weakness is a sign that he does not have the Spirit (10:1, 2).
Yet since they are undeserved gifts and did not happen
because of any human merit of Paul's, he speaks of them
as though another had had them, and declines to boast on
his own behalf. Of his own life, he prefers to boast only in
weaknesses. Paul's opponents may think that one is
proved to be a true disciple of Christ by his "visions and
revelations." Paul knows that one is proved to be true to
him by **weaknesses,** including suffering, for Christ himself was "crucified in weakness" (13:4). Paul's weaknesses
here may refer also to his "thorn in the flesh" (vs. 7),
which kept him from becoming proud.

[6] Here Paul points to another reason for his reserve
about his revelations. Paul does not **boast** of this experi-

⁷ And to keep me from being too elated by the abundance of revelations, a thorn was given me in the flesh,
a messenger of Satan, to harass me, to keep me from
being too elated.

---

ence because his authority as an apostle should not rest
on mysterious, private experiences. A fraud could delude
people by making such claims, based on his spiritual experiences. Indeed, the opponents have advanced themselves by making claims of their gifts of the Spirit. But
Paul, although he has had private experiences of the Spirit
(vss. 2-4), prefers to base his claim on things they could
see and hear in him. In that way no fraud is possible.
What they have seen and heard is his "weakness" (see
vs. 5). They know that he continually carries in his body
"the death of Jesus" (4:10), for they have seen and heard
this conduct. The Corinthians could not very well have
ascertained who was the true apostle of Jesus on the basis
of private experiences each boasted about. There would
have been no way to judge. Paul, who is here defending
himself, places the argument on grounds where they can
judge: things they have seen and heard.

[7] That which Paul in verse 6 refrains from boasting
about is the **abundance of revelations.** The word for **abundance** (*huperbolē*) does not necessarily imply quantity;
indeed here the word probably means "outstanding quality" (Héring, p. 92). Paul has had **revelations** that were
of overwhelming quality. But the effect of such experiences can be negative rather than positive; they can cause
one to be **too elated** (*huperairomai*). **Elated** here does
not carry the positive connotation of one who is simply
joyful; the word refers to those who arrogantly lift themselves up. Gifts of the Spirit, which Paul's opponents
claim, have made them too **elated** or arrogant.

One cannot exalt himself without deposing God from
his place. Thus God has protected Paul from arrogance
by giving him **a thorn in the flesh.** Whatever this **thorn
in the flesh** was, Paul saw it as discipline from God. Obviously, Paul is telling us here about severe discomfort;

yet Paul is not inclined to question God's mercy. In fact, this pain results from God's mercy. God is protecting him from the sin of pride.

Much discussion has been given to the subject of the **thorn in the flesh.** Since Paul seldom gives autobiographical information, we know almost nothing from his other statements which can throw light on this passage. Paul's description of his ailment as **a thorn in the flesh** may have been suggested by a similar expression in Numbers 33:55. Some have thought that Paul is referring to the mental anguish which accompanied his ministry. There was indeed a "daily pressure" of "anxiety for the churches" (11:28). Another view is that the **thorn** was Paul's opponents who plagued him in his work. However, Paul seems to be speaking quite literally here of physical torment. He mentions a particular ailment in Galatians 4:13 and says that because of some "bodily ailment" he first preached to them. Conjectures have been numerous, but not very convincing. A very old tradition was that Paul suffered from epilepsy. Paul, however, never gives any such indication. Some have thought, on the basis of Galatians 6:11 ("see what large letters I am writing") and Galatians 4:15 ("if possible, you would have plucked out your eyes for me"), that Paul had in mind an offensive eye ailment. That the **thorn in the flesh** was a chronic and recurring ailment seems to be certain; the verb **to harass** is in the present tense and suggests a continual ailment. When Paul says that the thorn is from **Satan,** he is using a theme that is not uncommon in the Bible: that Satan is allowed to afflict the body (cf. Job 2:4, 5; 1 Cor. 5:5; 1 Tim. 1:20).

The best evidence of what Paul's **thorn in the flesh** was comes from his description of what it does. It has come **to harass** (*kolaphizō*) him. The verb translated **harass** also means "to buffet" (see 1 Cor. 4:11) or "strike." The same word is used to describe the punishment of Jesus (Mark 14:65), where "they began . . . to strike him." Paul's **thorn** is most likely the constant persecution which he has to endure for his faith. But when he is har-

⁸ Three times I besought the Lord about this, that it
should leave me; ⁹ but he said to me, "my grace is sufficient
for you, for my power is made perfect in weakness." I will
all the more gladly boast of my weaknesses, that the power
of Christ may rest upon me.

---

assed or "beaten," as the word suggests, he is only imitating his Lord, who accepted punishment from messengers of Satan. That Paul's **thorn** is persecution seems also
to be indicated in verse 10, where he says that he is "content with . . . persecutions."

His opponents have mistaken his **thorn in the flesh**
for weakness. What they have taken for weakness is really
God's way of strengthening Paul. The **thorn** is at the same
time from God and a **messenger from Satan.** Certain
powers over man are granted to Satan (see Job 2:12).
Yet Satan's powers remain within the realm of God's purpose. The purpose here is to keep Paul humble.

[8] Paul thought of how much more work he could
have done if it were not for his constant sufferings. Thus
he prayed or **besought the Lord about this.** The prayer
is to **the Lord.** Since in verse 9 the "power" is the "power
of Christ," this prayer is evidently addressed to Christ.
Prayer to Christ is not uncommon in the New Testament
(cf. 1 Thess. 3:12, 13; 1 Cor. 1:2; Acts 7:59). He is the
risen, exalted Lord who "intercedes for us" (Rom. 8:34;
cf. Heb. 7:25).

Paul knows the experience of unanswered prayer and
also the desire to avoid pain. Like Jesus in Gethsemane
(Mark 14:36), Paul prays that he might not have to experience suffering. But he learns that God's refusal may
be an answer.

[9] Paul's specific request was not granted. But he
received a better answer than the one he had wanted.
He is not to think of his ministry as dependent on his
own resources. He depends on God. At 2:16, Paul asked
the question, "Who is sufficient for these things?" The

10 For the sake of Christ, then, I am content with weaknesses, insults, hardships, persecutions, and calamities; for when I am weak, then I am strong.

---

implied answer is, "No one, except through God's power." Since "our sufficiency is from God" (3:5), Paul's thorn is to remind him that it is God's resources, working through this frail human vessel (4:7), that will be **sufficient**. The word **grace** is not used here in the sense which it frequently has of the gift of salvation. Here the word is synonymous with the word **power** (see 4:7). If Paul could have pointed to remarkable physical resources, the power of God in his life would not be obvious. God's power is manifested in **weaknesses**. Thus the ultimate of human weakness, the cross of Christ, was the opportunity for the **power** of God to be displayed at the resurrection (13:4). In the same way, the **weakness** which Paul's opponents have seen in him was really the opportunity for God's **grace**. Thus Paul no more asks for release from suffering, because suffering is no curse. He will gladly **boast** of his sufferings, knowing that they are useful in advancing God's purpose.

[10] Since Christ died for the sake of men (5:14), Paul is happy to undergo hardship **for the sake of Christ**. These hardships are the signs that he is a true apostle (cf. 6:4, 5). His opponents criticize his **weaknesses** (10:10), but he gladly boasts of it (cf. 11:30; 12:5) because Christ himself was weak (13:4).

Insults can refer to verbal attacks or to physical assaults. **Hardships** were mentioned at 6:4 as a sign of Paul's apostleship. Paul's **persecutions** were mentioned at 4:9; according to Mark 10:30, **persecutions** are to be expected for Jesus' disciples until the end. **Calamities** are mentioned at 6:4 (cf. 4:8). The word suggests an "impasse," where it looks as if no answer was to be found.

Verse 10b sums up the idea of verses 9 and 10a with a "magnificent aphorism" (Héring). The expression is paradoxical, but true. Only when he is **weak** in human

175

¹¹ **I have been a fool! You forced me to it, for I ought to have been commended by you. For I am not at all inferior to these superlative apostles, even though I am nothing.** ¹² **The signs of a true apostle were performed among you in all patience, with signs and wonders and mighty works.**

---

resources is he **strong** in divine power. The statement is an apt commentary on Philippians 4:13: "I can do all things through Christ who strengthens me."

Paul's Work As His Recommendation, 12:11-16

[11] Paul knows that such boasting of outward things is foolish (see 11:21). If the Corinthians had not failed in their loyalty to him, his boasting would have been unnecessary. Paul should not need to commend himself as the false teachers do (3:1; 5:12). The Corinthians, having seen his dedication and his endurance, were in a position to commend him. They are his converts, and thus, his "letter of recommendation" (3:2). But instead, they listened to the **superlative apostles** and **forced** Paul into boasting.

The RSV **I am not at all inferior** has the wrong tense; the aorist tense of the verb for "be inferior" (*husterēsa*) indicates that at a specific time, i.e., when Paul was in Corinth, he was inferior in no way. Paul is **nothing** because all of his work was due to God's grace (see vs. 9; 1 Cor. 15:9).

[12] Paul is not inferior to the superlative apostles (11:5) because he was able to equal any miracles that they performed. The false teachers look upon miraculous powers as the proof of true apostleship and thus commend themselves by miraculous gifts. When Paul speaks of the **signs of a true apostle,** he is probably using the language of false teachers who have called themselves "true apostles." Miracles, according to them, serve as proof of one's apostleship. Thus Paul finds it necessary here, as at 11:22 and 12:1ff., to argue on their level. Paul

¹³ For in what were you less favored than the rest of the churches, except that I myself did not burden you. Forgive me this wrong!

---

does not necessarily look upon miracles as proof of apostleship, but since the false teachers boast about their miracles, Paul argues on their terms.

It is to be noted that Paul uses the passive voice when describing his miracles. These **signs . . . were performed**, but Paul does not take the credit; God was the source of such signs. The signs were performed **in all patience** (*hupomonē*). **Signs** (*sēmeion*) is used frequently in the New Testament for miraculous activity. (see Mark 8:11); in the Gospel of John the word is used almost exclusively for Jesus' miracles (cf. John 2:11; 18, 23; 4:54; 6:2). **Signs and wonders and mighty works** do not refer to different categories of miracles. All three words are used to designate miraculous activity in the New Testament. This threefold formula is found also in one other place in the New Testament (Acts 2:22). Miracles in the New Testament centered around works of healing, although the Gospels record several "nature miracles" (cf. Mark 4:35-41; 8:1-11), which give evidence of God's power over nature. The New Testament approaches this miraculous content with considerable reserve. Jesus is never depicted as the kind of wonder-worker who performed miracles only to show his power. His miracles were signs that the kingdom was at hand (Luke 11:20).

Paul's reference to his miraculous activity raises the question of what place these **signs and wonders and mighty works** had in his ministry. Only here and at Galatians 3:5 and Romans 15:19 does Paul refer to his miraculous works (see Heb. 2:4). Thus it seems apparent that, although Paul performed miracles, he did not place much emphasis on this activity. Wonder-workers were common, and consequently Paul does not appeal to his miracles as proof of his apostleship.

[13] Paul's opponents accept pay for their work. Apparently they place such an importance on the church's

¹⁴ Here for the third time I am ready to come to you. And I will not be a burden, for I seek not what is yours but you; for children ought not to lay up for their parents, but parents for children.

responsibility to support an "apostle" that it is considered an offense when the apostle does not accept support. The false teachers have accused Paul of "sin" (11:7) in not accepting support. The Corinthians feel that they were **less favored** or "inferior" because they have not given support to Paul, and it is Paul's fault. Paul caused them to be remiss in their responsibilities and is guilty of a **wrong** (*adikia,* "unrighteousness"; see 11:7). The words **I myself** mean "I alone." Paul is contrasting himself to the false teachers, who "make slaves" of the Corinthians by demanding support. With bitter irony Paul says, **Forgive me this wrong!** The selflessness with which he had tried to maintain good relations with them had been distorted. At the very point where he had tried to be gracious to them, they had accused him of wrong. Here was one of the deepest of Paul's discouragements.

[14] Both here and at 13:1 Paul mentions his prospective visit (see Introduction). The first visit is recorded in Acts 18:1. Paul founded the church there on his second missionary journey. The second visit is mentioned at 2:1; it was the "painful visit," when Paul attempted to put down a rebellion. He will not **burden** them, as the false teachers do; he will follow his custom of supporting himself. His statement, **I seek not what is yours, but you,** is an implied contrast to his opponents. Paul is concerned only with their loyalty to Christ. That loyalty will restore friendly relationships between Paul and them.

His unselfish interest in them fulfills a natural law of human life: **children** are not expected to care for their **parents**; rather, **parents** must provide for the needs of their **children** without thought of repayment. Paul thinks of himself in a most intimate relation to the Corinthians. Here he is the parent. At 11:2, he is the father of the

¹⁵ I will most gladly spend and be spent for your souls.
If I love you the more, am I to be loved the less? ¹⁶ But
granting that I myself did not burden you, I was crafty,
you say, and got the better of by guile.

---

bride who "betrothed" his daughter to Christ. Paul does
not mean that children should never do anything for
parents but that it is natural for parents to bring up children in the spirit of unselfish giving and not ask for financial support.

If Paul had observed this rule strictly, he would never
have accepted support from other churches; yet we know
that he did accept gifts from other churches to support
him while he was at Corinth (11:7-9). Here he means
simply that, since the Christians there are his children,
he is happy to work without receiving any support from
them.

[15] Paul is like a good parent who will sacrifice for
his children. Thus he says, **I will most gladly spend and
be spent for your souls.** The idea sounds similar to Mark
10:45: "The Son of Man came . . . to give his life a ran-
som for many." Paul learned from the cross of Jesus that
one who accepts Christ can no longer live for himself
(5:15). Thus Paul lives in imitation of Christ; his whole
life is a self-sacrifice for their souls. Because he lives for
others, he is more concerned to **spend** and **be spent** than
to receive. He depletes every physical and mental resource
he has for others.

Verse 15b is the answer to the question which was
raised at 11:11. His motives have been misunderstood
(see 11:7-10). His sign of great love (that he did not accept support) was taken by them to be a sign of less love,
indeed a "sin" (11:7). The question here is an appeal
for understanding. He hopes that they will see his **love**
and respond with more **love.**

[16] Paul pursues every accusation that has been made
against him in order to clear himself. His opponents say
that Paul did not accept money in order that he might by

179

[17] Did I take advantage of you through any of those whom I sent you? [18] I urged Titus to go, and sent the brother with him. Did Titus take advantage of you? Did we not act in the same Spirit? Did we not take the same steps?

---

guile take advantage of them. He was, according to them, **crafty** enough to get his money in other ways. **Crafty** (*panourgos*) means literally, "capable of doing anything." At 11:3 the word is used of Satan's "cunning." That Paul has been accused of taking advantage of the Corinthians is evident from 4:2 and 7:2.

[17] Paul wants to end all the charges against him. One charge is that, although he did not personally exploit them, he used his associates for that task. The question here implies that Paul frequently sent messengers to Corinth to carry letters and to help the church there. Paul's associates never "made slaves" (see 11:20) of them, as did Paul's opponents.

[18] The reputation of **Titus** has remained unblemished in Corinth. It is Titus who had brought back the encouraging news of their repentance (7:5) and who was willingly coming again to them to take the collection. The **brother** who remains nameless (see 8:22 and comments on that passage) must also have been of unimpeachable integrity. Mention of the trip of **Titus** and the **brother** has made it appear plausible that Paul is discussing the trip which he mentions at 8:16-22. If so, chapters 10—13 would be separate from and later than 1—9. But Titus made more than one trip to Corinth (cf. 8:6; 2:13; 7:6). When could Titus have taken **advantage** of the Corinthians? Paul is probably referring to the time when Titus **made a beginning** on the collection (8:6). It is possible here that Titus' part in the collection may have given occasion for some to implicate both Titus and Paul in an accusation of their motives. Thus Paul appeals here to Titus' reputation. Titus had a good reputation, as Paul knows. Paul reminds the Corinthians that he acted in the **same spirit** and took the **same steps** as did Titus. Therefore, the possibility that Paul acted with "guile" (vs. 16) is precluded.

¹⁹ Have you been thinking all along that we have been defending ourselves before you? It is in the sight of God that we have been speaking in Christ, and all for your upbuilding, beloved. ²⁰ For I fear that perhaps I may come and find you not what I wish, and that you may find me not what you wish; that perhaps there may be quarreling, jealousy, anger, selfishness, slander, gossip, conceit, and disorder.

Appeal to Repent before Paul Comes, 12:19—13:10

[19] Paul is concerned here lest the Corinthians think that his only purpose in this discussion is to defend himself. It is unquestionable that Paul has been **defending** himself. But his interest is not in mere self-vindication. He is concerned to bring about the **upbuilding** of the church. He has been **defending** himself as an apostle so that they will take the right attitude in order that he will not have to discipline them when he comes. He is speaking **in the sight of God** as a man **in Christ**; he is not afraid of divine scrutiny. His honesty is assured by his relationship to Christ (see 2:17).

[20] In this and the next verse Paul tells why he has spoken so earnestly in his own defense. Before Paul can resume a healthy relationship with them, they need upbuilding (vs. 19). This upbuilding can come about by putting away their unchristian behavior. The list of vices resembles closely the "works of the flesh" mentioned in Galatians 5:19, 20. We find lists of vices to be avoided by Christian people in many places in the New Testament (cf. Eph. 5:3-8; Col. 3:5-9; Rom. 1:28ff.), as are lists of virtues (Col. 3:12ff.; Gal. 5:22ff.; Eph. 4:25ff.). Lists could very easily be committed to memory, and so the lists were a favorite teaching device whereby new converts learned of their responsibilities as Christians. Paul mentions this list of vices which the Corinthians had long ago been told to put away; he is afraid that when he comes he will find them still needing the upbuilding that can come only when they put away these vices. **Quarreling** (*eris*) had

²¹ I fear that when I come again my God may humble
me before you, and I may have to mourn over many of
those who sinned before and have not repented of the
impurity, immorality, and licentiousness which they have
practiced.

---

been with the Corinthians since before Paul wrote 1 Corinthians (see 1 Cor. 1:11); it is a sign of immaturity. The
word for **jealousy** (*zēlos*) means "a passionate commitment." The same word is used in the sense of "zeal" in
11:3. Here the word signifies the "passionate commitment"
to have what belongs to someone else (see Gal. 5:20).
Anger (*thumoi*) is "uncontrolled temper" which at times
"boils over." **Selfishness** (*eritheia*) is a "work of the flesh"
(Gal. 5:20); it signifies the man who has no conception
of living for others. **Slander** (*katalalia*, "to speak against")
is any kind of hostile speech. The New Testament emphasizes strongly the necessity of avoiding this sin. It is
taken for granted that pagans **slander** (see 1 Peter 2:1);
but Christians are to do away with this sin (cf. James
4:11; Rom. 1:30; 1 Peter 2:2ff.). **Gossip** (*psithurismoi*) is
any kind of tale-bearing (see Rom. 1:29). **Conceit** (*phusio-
seis*) is "swellings" caused by one's sense of his own importance. **Disorders** (*akatastasia*) are "tumults" or "insur-
rections" which have no place in the church, since God is
not a God of confusion, but of peace (1 Cor. 14:33). Paul
is thus afraid that upon coming he will find a church lacking any signs of the Spirit's presence among them. If he
finds them in such a poor condition, he will see the failure of much of his labor.

[21] Paul in verse 20 lists sins which can be listed
under the general heading "party spirit" or "disorder." At
verse 21, he lists three sexual sins. Lists of vices usually
gave reference to sins both of "party spirit" and of a
sexual nature (see Gal. 5:20). First Corinthians leaves no
doubt that the Corinthians had lived with great sexual
license before they became Christians (see 1 Cor. 6:9);
Paul had shown great concern over their sexual morality
(1 Cor. 6; 7). In this passage we find an indication that

¹ **This is the third time I am coming to you. Any charge must be sustained by the evidence of two or three witnesses.**

some of the Christians in Corinth were still living sexually immoral lives. Perhaps the false teachers had unintentionally given a fresh occasion and excuse to those who had earlier been rebuked by Paul for sexual license. The problem does not seem to be widespread at Corinth at this time, or Paul would have discussed it more at length. It is a serious problem, nevertheless. These three overlapping words for sexual license are found in Galatians 5:20. **Impurity** (*akatharsia*) can be used either with or without a sexual connotation; it describes the opposite of purity, which is characteristic of the Christian's state of being set apart for sanctification. **Immorality** (*porneia*, "fornication") is the word for "every kind of unlawful sexual intercourse" (Arndt and Gingrich). The Corinthians lived in a pagan environment which did not frown on adultery; it was expected for a man to take his pleasures wherever he could. In this environment, such a relapse was a constant temptation for Christians. **Uncleanness** (*aselgeia*) does not solely refer to sexual uncleanness. It is wanton, unrestrained, or indecent behavior.

How does Paul expect to be humbled? God will **humble** Paul by allowing him to accept defeat here. The unrepentant offenders will not be restored, and this will be Paul's humiliation. He will have to **mourn over** them as spiritually lost or dead.

[1] Paul has already warned his readers of the impending third visit (12:14a; see Introduction). He does not want it to turn out like his second "painful visit" (2:1; 13:2). There has been considerable improvement since that visit (see 7:5ff.), but the influence of the false teachers is still felt in Corinth. The reference to **two or three witnesses** is an allusion to Deuteronomy 19:15, which gives as a rule for judicial proceedings that a charge can only be sustained against a man when there are **two or three witnesses**. The same passage is alluded to in Mat-

² I warned those who sinned before and all the others, and I warn them now while absent, as I did when present on my second visit, that if I come again, I will not spare them—

---

thew 18:16; there it is a rule for relations between disciples that two or three witnesses must be heard before an accusation can stand.

Does Paul allude to this passage on judicial proceedings in order to indicate that when he comes he will conduct a trial, complete with witnesses? Since the offenders are well known, it is doubtful that such witnesses for convicting guilty persons are needed. As verse 2 indicates, Paul will indeed inflict punishment when he comes; but it is unlikely that he will need witnesses, since the guilt is already well known. The connection between Paul's impending visit and the two or three witnesses is the number three. Mention of the third visit reminds Paul of the rule that two or three witnesses are necessary in judicial proceedings. Each visit for Paul was a witness. His third visit will be the third witness. He has given them time to repent. Now he will inflict punishment after allowing them three witnesses (or visits).

[2] Paul's opponents have said that Paul is more stern in his letters than he is in person (10:11). Paul assures his readers that when he comes, they will see that he can be as authoritative in person as he is in his letters. He warned them on his second visit there (2:1), but took no action. His failure to take action may have given the impression that he lacked the authority to take action. Now he will not spare or "restrain himself" from taking action. Paul had once before planned to go to Corinth, but he decided not to go in order to spare them (1:23). He has given them ample opportunity to repent.

From what punishment does Paul intend to spare his opponents? Verse 10 mentions the possibility that Paul will be "severe" in his use of authority when he comes. It is conceivable here that Paul has in mind exclusion from the fellowship. One offender has already been punished

[3] **since you desire proof that Christ is speaking in me. He is not weak in dealing with you, but is powerful in you.**

"by the majority" (2:6) for his part in revolting against Paul on his second visit to them. An immoral man was to be punished from the fellowship for his behavior, according to 1 Corinthians 5:5. It is to be noticed in this passage that whatever punishment is to be exercised, Paul will do it singlehandedly (**I will not spare them**). If he is talking of excluding the sinners from the fellowship, he cannot act without the cooperation of "the majority" (see 2:6). Therefore, it is probable that Paul is talking of something more than exclusion from the fellowship, since he is acting alone. A miraculous punishment is a more likely punishment here. Paul has tried exclusion from the fellowship (2:5ff.); now on his third visit he will be more severe. What form such miraculous punishment could take is not known; one may compare two other instances in the New Testament where miraculous punishment is given (Acts 5:1ff.; 13:9ff.). It is this kind of punishment which may have been given to the immoral man who was "delivered to Satan" (1 Cor. 5:5). One may compare also the sickness and death that befell those in Corinth who did not partake of the Lord's Supper in the right way (1 Cor. 11:29).

[3] Because Paul's speech is "of no account," his opponents conclude that he lacks any spiritual gifts, such as the gift of speech. They want **proof** that Christ speaks in Paul. The **proof** which the opponents demand is an example of **power.** They demanded **proof** of Paul's relationship to Christ because they saw only "weakness" in him. Now they want some decisive action as a sign. Paul's claim here is not that he has great powers, but that the Lord, working through Paul, is **powerful.** He never boasts of himself, as the opponents do; he only boasts of what the Lord does through him (10:17, 18). If they are impressed by power, they will see the Lord's power on Paul's third visit. This power will be the punishment which they will receive when he does not "spare" them (vs. 2).

⁴ For he was crucified in weakness, but lives by the power of God. For we are weak in him, but in dealing with you we shall live with him by the power of God.

⁵ Examine yourselves, to see whether you are holding to your faith. Test yourselves. Do you not realize that Jesus Christ is in you?—unless indeed you fail to meet the test!

---

[4] At the crucifixion, sin seemed victorious. It seemed to expose the weakness of Christ. From a mere human point of view the idea of a crucified savior was a "stumbling block to Jews" (1 Cor. 1:23), since Jews "demand signs" (1 Cor. 1:22) of power. Paul's opponents, being Jewish Christians, preach "another Jesus" (11:4); they place emphasis on Jesus the wonder-worker but not as one who was crucified in weakness (see comments on 5:16ff.). The power which Paul describes comes only in the midst of weakness (12:9). If the cross was the epitome of weakness, the resurrection was the epitome of God's power. Christ lives by the power of God. The New Testament speaks frequently of the resurrection as the chief example of God's power. "God raised the Lord and will raise us by his power" (1 Cor. 6:14; cf. Rom. 1:4).

Paul's opponents have accused him of weakness. He freely admits and even boasts of this (11:30), for in weakness he is united with him. In baptism he has been buried with him (Rom. 6:4) so he could share in Christ's "newness of life." To be with him is to share completely the life which Jesus knew: the road from weakness to glory. The only way to power for Jesus was the path of weakness; Paul therefore follows the Lord in sharing his weakness. The result is that he shares his power. The power of his resurrection is available to Paul as he shares the sufferings of Christ (Phil. 3:10; cf. Eph. 1:19, 20). Thus when Paul exercises discipline on the church there, his power is nothing less than the power of God.

[5] Verse 5 urges the readers to practice "self-criticism" to see if they are living by the standard Paul has stated in verse 4. They should examine themselves and test

themselves because Paul will soon come to test them. If they are to **meet the test,** they must repent before Paul arrives by putting away those sins mentioned in 12:20-21 and by withdrawing from the troublemakers. There is no essential difference of meaning here between **examine** (*peirazete*) and **test** (*dokimazete*). The noun form for **test** (*dokimē*) is translated "proof" in verse 3 (see comments on 2:9). The Corinthians have tested Paul by the standard they considered important: his power. They have demanded "proof" that Christ spoke through Paul (vs. 3), i.e., they have given him a test. Now Paul is declaring with emphasis: you keep attempting to test me; you keep suspecting my work and belittling me; now you must **test yourselves.** In Greek, **yourselves** is placed before the words **examine** and **test** in order to emphasize that it is they, not Paul, who are on trial.

The purpose of the examination is to see if they are **holding to the faith. Faith** in the New Testament most commonly is an attitude of trust in God (see 2 Cor. 5:7). Here the word is used in a different sense. To be in the faith is to stand in a relationship to Jesus Christ, to be "a new creature" (5:17) in him. One is to "stand firm in the faith" (1 Cor. 16:13); Paul encourages his readers in Colossians to "continue in the faith, stable and steadfast" (Col. 1:23). Paul recognizes here in all of these exhortations about standing firm in the faith that Christ can impart, that they can "fall from grace." Here we notice that to be in the faith is equivalent to the expression **Christ is in you** (see Col. 2:7, "rooted and built up in him and established in the faith"). Paul affirms elsewhere (Gal. 2:20; Col. 1:27) that Christ lives in the Christian.

There remains the possibility that the readers will **fail to meet the test** which Paul gives. What is this **test**—to determine whether or not they are in the faith or that Christ is in them? Verse 4 gives part of the answer. Christ was crucified in weakness and raised by God's power. Paul gives proof that Christ is in him by living as Christ lived: in weakness. He commends himself, not by his power but by his suffering (6:4ff.). He daily bears the sufferings of

⁶ I hope you will find out that we have not failed. ⁷ But we pray God that you may not do wrong—not that we may appear to have met the test, but that you may do what is right, though we may seem to have failed. ⁸ For we cannot do anything against the truth, but only for the truth.

Jesus, and thus manifests the life of Jesus in his flesh (4:10, 11). Christ lives in Paul because Paul has been crucified with Christ (Gal. 2:20). The test which the Corinthians may not meet is the test of one's willingness to suffer with Christ and accept his weakness (vs. 3). They have used the wrong standard in demanding proof from Paul (vs. 3). Now he will test them.

[6] Paul has indeed passed the real test because he has imitated Jesus' sufferings; Christ is in him. He hopes now that the Corinthians will see that he has not failed the test which they are giving (vs. 3). They will find out that Paul is a genuine apostle when they realize that the weakness which they criticize (10:10) is really proof that Christ is in Paul (4:10, 11; 13:13). When they realize what the real standard is, they will accept his leadership.

[7] Paul's great concern is not for his own success or reputation. It is that the Corinthians may not do wrong. Even his hope, expressed in verse 6, that they learn that he is a true minister of Jesus Christ, is not selfish. If the Corinthians do right, Paul himself may look like a failure; if they do wrong, Paul will have met the test. That is, only in their wrongdoing will Paul have opportunity to give proof (vs. 3) which they have demanded of him to show that he is a true apostle. But Paul is willing to let the proof of his authority remain in abeyance. There is something more important than vindicating himself; that is to see the Corinthians do right. One may compare Paul's unselfish spirit here with Romans 9:3; in that passage Paul is so involved with his ministry that what happens to him is unimportant as compared with his concern for the spiritual progress of others.

[8] Paul does not mean here that it is impossible for

⁹ **For we are glad when we are weak and you are strong. What we pray for is your improvement. ¹⁰ I write this while I am away from you, in order that when I come I may not have to be severe in my use of the authority which the Lord has given me for building up and not for tearing down.**

him to oppose the truth. Verse 7 provides a key to understanding this verse. To act against the truth would be to bring in the element of personal satisfaction, mentioned in verse 7. The very nature of the message entrusted to Paul demands that he subordinate personal satisfaction to the progress of the gospel. Truth here means "true teaching," in contrast to a "different gospel" (11:4). Paul's ministry is the "open statement of the truth" (4:2). Since he is in the service of God's revelation of truth, it would be completely out of character for him to be concerned about his private satisfaction.

[9] Verse 9 is an apt conclusion to the thoughts of 1-8. It is to be remembered that his opponents have accused him of being weak (10:10). In this case, Paul may appear to be weak to his opponents if he does not back up his threats and exercise strict discipline (see vs. 2). If now they will become strong, i.e., if they will "do what is right" (vs. 7), Paul will be glad to appear weak. He will gladly forego exercising discipline, even if it makes him look weak. Evidence that they are strong will be shown in their willingness to expel the offenders (see 6:14f.) and to put away those sins listed at 12:20, 21.

Here, as in verse 7, Paul mentions his prayer for them. He prays for their improvement (*katartisin*). The KJV translates the word "perfection." The word has the meaning of "confirmed" or "firmly grounded" in Christian character or in faith (see 1 Thess. 3:10). In Luke 6:40, the goal of the Christian life is to be "fully taught."

[10] Paul's opponents have charged that his letters were "weighty and strong" (10:10) but that in person he was weak, i.e., he would not carry out his threats. Here Paul explains why he frightens them with letters (10:9).

¹¹ Finally, brethren, farewell. Mend your ways, heed my appeal, agree with one another, live in peace, and the God of love and peace will be with you.

The Lord has indeed given Paul **authority** (see 10:8) which can be used either **for building up** or **for tearing down**. But **authority** presupposes a responsible use; one who keeps in mind that his **authority** is from Christ for the growth of the church will not use his authority rashly for self-vindication. Thus Paul could impress the Corinthians with his strength if he used his authority to tear down; but in **tearing down** he would neglect the purpose of his ministry.

The idea of **building up** is a metaphor taken from the activity of building houses or temples and other buildings. In the New Testament this metaphor is useful in describing the church as something which is in the process of being built. Thus Jesus "will build the church" (Matt. 16:18). Paul, as apostle, laid the foundation at Corinth, and others built upon it (1 Cor. 3:10-15). Paul's major concern is the upbuilding of the church (1 Cor. 12:19; cf. 14:3). All Christian behavior is to be tested by whether or not it leads to the upbuilding of the church (cf. 1 Cor. 8:1; 10:23). Thus Paul by **tearing down** might have satisfied a selfish impulse; but as an apostle his only interest is in **building up** what in the long run will be a stronger church.

CONCLUSION AND BENEDICTION, 13:11-14

At verse 11, Paul begins to give the closing exhortations and greetings. We noticed previously that Paul always employs the same general introduction to his epistles (see comments on 1:1). His concluding remarks generally follow the same form also. Paul usually concludes with a greeting and an exhortation (cf. 1 Cor. 16:15ff.; Gal. 6:16-18; Eph. 6:23, 24), followed by a closing benediction similar to 13:14.

[11] **Mend your ways** is the translation for the same

¹² **Greet one another with a holy kiss.**

---

word which is in verse 9 translated "improvement." Paul
exhorts them to put away quarreling and sexual sins (cf.
12:20, 21) and to become more fully grounded in their
relationship to Christ. The word can either mean "mend
yourselves" or "be mended." **Heed my appeal** can either
mean "encourage one another," as in 1 Thessalonians 5:11,
or be an encouragement for the Corinthians to **heed** what
Paul has said, as the RSV translates. In view of what follows, Paul seems to be appealing to them to encourage
each other, so as to build up the church. **Agree with one
another** can also be translated "be of the same mind" or
"live in harmony" (cf. Rom. 15:5; Phil. 2:2). It is an appeal for the Corinthians to give up the divisive spirit
which had been chronic there (see 1 Cor. 1:10ff.). Christ
established **peace** at the cross (Eph. 2:14), but the church
must maintain this peace (Eph. 4:3). The result of living
in harmony and **peace** is that **the God of love and peace
will be with you.** These words are both a benediction and
a promise. The word **and** implies, "and then, if you do
these things constantly." God is elsewhere called "the God
of peace" (Rom. 15:33; Phil. 4:9). Love is mentioned as
an attribute of God in other places in the New Testament
(see Rom. 5:8); only here, however, does Paul use the
expression **the God of love.** The effect of being at peace
with God is that the church will be reconciled. When
members have received the peace and love of God, they
in turn are at peace as a community.

[12] The **holy kiss** as a form of Christian greeting is
found frequently in the New Testament (cf. Acts 20:37;
Rom. 16:16; 1 Cor. 16:20; 1 Thess. 5:26; 1 Peter 5:14).
The kiss was recognized among Jews as a sign of reconciliation (Héring, p. 103), and so it was natural that this
act symbolize a Christian greeting. It is generally called
a **holy** (*hagios*) kiss (see 1 Peter 5:14, "kiss of love") because it was exchanged by the saints (*hagioi*). Luke 7:45
seems to indicate that the kiss was valued by Jesus. The
fact that Judas chose the kiss to enable his company to

¹³ All the saints greet you.

¹⁴ And the grace of the Lord Jesus Christ and the love of God and the fellowship ⁿ of the Holy Spirit be with you all.

ⁿ Or *and participation in*

---

identify Jesus indicates that it was in frequent use by Jesus and the disciples. The practice continued to be widespread in the second century churches, where it was accepted with the caution that it be practiced only between man and man and woman and woman.

[13] **All the saints** are all of the Christians in the place from which Paul is writing. According to 7:5ff., this place is Macedonia. (On **saints**, see comments on 1:1.)

[14] This is the most elaborate benediction in any of Paul's letters, and the only one which mentions together God, Christ, and the Holy Spirit. Thus Paul's only concern here is not in speculating about the Trinity but in describing the practical effects of God's work in the Christian life. **Grace** is the undeserved gift of salvation. It is the "grace of God" (Acts 13:43) and the **grace of the Lord Jesus Christ** (2 Cor. 8:9). Paul frequently refers to the grace of Christ in his benedictions (cf. 1 Cor. 16:23; 1 Thess. 5:28; Rom. 16:20). This **grace of the Lord Jesus Christ** is granted to all Christians. Not only is it a once-for-all gift of salvation, it is also a daily gift to the believer (8:1, 7). **The love of God** is the active good will by which he saved us "while we were yet sinners" (Rom. 5:8). The love is made known through Jesus Christ, and continues to strengthen the believer (Rom. 8:32). **The fellowship of the Holy Spirit** may refer either to the spirit of fellowship which the presence of the Holy Spirit creates, as the parallel with the other phrases suggests, or to the fact that Christians together share or participate in the Holy Spirit. **Fellowship** is usually a "sharing in" the object ("his sufferings," Phil. 3:10; "his body and blood," 1 Cor. 10:16). Thus **the fellowship of the Holy Spirit** is the joint participation of the church in God's Spirit.